D O R S

NATIONAL T... ...

W·A·L·K·S

Rodney Legg

This selection from Rodney Legg's acclaimed series of circular country walks, a model of their kind, comes from the popular publications *Dorset County Magazine* and *Dorset Life*. They also appear in Dorset's first all-colour magazine — *Dorset: The Magazine For People Who Like To Explore*

dpc

DORSET PUBLISHING COMPANY
at the WINCANTON PRESS NATIONAL SCHOOL
NORTH STREET WINCANTON SOMERSET BA9 9AT

For **Roger Chorley**
who enjoyed my Purbeck collection

Country walking
ROUTES — These are described as found at the time the
specific walk was researched. They are along public rights of
way and public roads, or across land where the public has
freedom to roam, such as certain common land and at
National Trust properties. All paths are liable to changes —
from natural causes, agricultural practices and legal
diversions.

PROBLEMS EN ROUTE — Carry secateurs so that you can
clip your way through any offending vegetation. More serious
obstructions should be bypassed and their presence reported
to the local highway authority. Likewise other difficulties.
Contact the Rights of Way Office, Transportation and
Engineering Department, Dorset County Council, County Hall,
Dorchester, Dorset DT1 1XJ. Switchboard: 01-305-251-000.
Direct Line: 01-305-224-463. Fax: 01-305-224-835.

Publishing details
First published 1997. Copyright Rodney Legg © 1997
Published by Dorset Publishing Company at the Wincanton Press, National School, North
Street, Wincanton, Somerset BA9 9AT (01-963-325-83) to whom updatings may be sent,
addressed to the author. Distribution by Halsgrove, Lower Moor Way, Tiverton, Devon
EX16 6SS (01-884-243-242)

Printing credits
Typeset by Maurice Hann. Printed in Somerset by F. W. B. Printing, Bennetts Mead,
Southgate Road, Wincanton, Somerset BA9 9EB (01-963-337-55)

International standard book number
ISBN 0 948699 63 9

Contents

LAMBERT'S CASTLE & TEMPEST COTTAGE, pages 5 to 10
(6 miles: far western hills)

STONEBARROW HILL & GOLDEN CAP, pages 11 to 15
(5 miles: ascent from the west)

GOLDEN CAP & SEATOWN, pages 16 to 21
(5 miles: highest cliff on the South Coast)

THORNCOMBE BEACON & EYPE DOWN, pages 22 to 26
(5 miles: rugged western seascape)

EGGARDON & POWERSTOCK COMMON, pages 27 to 30
(7 miles: hill-fort and wilderness)

SWYRE & PUNCKNOWLE, pages 31 to 36
(5 miles: Chesil Beach hinterland)

OLD HARRY ROCKS & STUDLAND, pages 37 to 41
(5 miles: famous chalk cliffs)

SCOTLAND & PURBECK'S TEXAS, pages 42 to 48
(6 miles: backwaters of Poole Harbour)

MORETON & CLOUDS HILL, pages 49 to 53
(4 miles: Frome valley heathland)

BADBURY RINGS & LODGE FARM, page 54 to 59
(4 miles: hill-fort country)

STOURPAINE & HOD HILL, pages 60 to 65
(4 miles: hill-fort above the Stour)

FONTMELL DOWN & MELBURY BEACON, pages 66 to 70
(5 miles: pillars of chalk)

**Glimpses of Dorset: illustrations
by Joseph Pennell from 1906**

Lambert's Castle
& Tempest Cottage

Lambert's Castle is the last in the string of romantic hills that are the northern sentinals to the Marshwood Vale. Crossed but not spoilt by the B3165, it rises five miles north-east of Lyme Regis and has literally gone in and out of the counties of Devon and Dorset. Historically it was part of the Dorset parish of Hawkchurch and was lost with that village to Devon in the nineteenth century but the hilltop would be regained and added to the Dorset parish of Marshwood in a 1960s boundary change.

From 842 feet, the views cover most of west Dorset to the Chesil Beach and Portland with glimpses through the trees westwards to Dartmoor. These heavily wooded north-west slopes are the most westerly beech woods in Dorset. The south-west part of the plateau is common land with unfenced roads and patches of gorse and heather, studded with tussocks of purple moor grass (*Molina caerulea*) — a piece of relict landscape that has gone from common-place to rarity in our time. Both contrasting ecosystems are included in the 167 acres that were given to the National Trust by Lieutenant-Colonel (Alfred) Douglas Pass of Wootton Manor in 1956. The Trust has since acquired additional fields.

"Lamberht" — a Saxon personal name — became "Labirihtes Gete" for the gap in the hills, as with Corfe Gate being the name for the pass at Corfe Castle in the Purbeck Hills. The north end of the hill is entrenched with a single bank Iron Age hillfort of about 400 to 300 BC. It would have been palisaded and the rampart is a good deal higher than the interior but the outer ditch is the best preserved feature. It is unexcavated but is probably earlier than the much more elaborate fortifications on nearby Pilsdon Pen.

In the Middle Ages it was almost certainly used as a beacon site and from 1709 to 1947 the earthworks were utilised for an annual fair. This took place on the Wednesday preceding John the Baptist's day [24th June] and the site of the Fair House is immediately inside the fort entrance on the right hand side. Other low earthworks mark the sites of stalls and sheep enclosures. Horse races were part of the fair and the racecourse was a circuit of the open hilltop south of the fort. For a time, in the nineteenth century, a second fair was held in September.

On the flat top of the hillfort, east from the centre at a point 220 feet from the entrance, is a mound which is the site of a shutter-telegraph built by George Roebuck in the winter of 1805-06. The system which crossed Dorset was known as the Plymouth Line. Lookouts used telescopes to watch the next station in each direction, which from here were Toller Down to the east and Dalwood Common in the west. Roebuck's system was built at the height of the Napoleonic wars in the months after the Battle of Trafalgar.

A warning of invasion in the West Country could have been transmitted to the Admiralty in Whitehall in about thirty minutes — provided that it happened on a clear day. Often, however, these western hills have their heads in the clouds. In 1822 the stations were converted to a simpler semaphore system devised by Sir Home Riggs Popham. That would be replaced by the Electric Telegraph in 1847 and these watching posts were then abandoned.

A mile south-west along the ridge, towards Lyme Regis, is Tempest Cottage. The building is pleasant but unexceptional; modern rendering and tiles, two storeys, with older style flint-like chunks of chert in the rear walls. What is unusual, however, is its name. This is a link with the adventures of Sir George Somers [1554-1610] and the *Sea Venture*, which was wrecked in 1609 on an uninhabited chain of islands in the mid-Atlantic, leading to an account the following year of *A Discovery of the Bermudas, otherwise called the Isle of Devils.*

The author was Silvester Jourdain, who was born in these hills and sailed from Lyme Regis. Somers was also a west Dorset mariner and his embalmed body would be brought home by his nephew, Matthew Somers, for a military funeral in the church at Whitchurch Canonicorum. Meanwhile, a copy of the *Discovery of the Bermudas* found its way to William Shakespeare who was inspired to write *The Tempest*, which had its first performance in 1611.

Tempest Cottage was evidently the home of seafaring chronicler Silvester Jourdain.

In the tumbled landscape below where the great one hundred and sixty feet pylons of the national grid stride out of the Marshwood Vale, landscape painter Lucien Pissarro [1863-1944], son of famous impressionist Camille Pissarro, had a cottage in Fishpond Bottom. His work there included *Road from the Hill, Fishpond* and *Dorset Garden*. James Manson, the director of the Tate Gallery, frequently shared Pissarro's rural retreat. They maintained a correspondence for 35 years which survives in its entirety in the Ashmolean Museum, Oxford. "They went painting together whenever they could," daughter Mary Manson told me in 1977.

On the other side of Fishpond, Coney's Castle is a double-banked Iron Age hill-fort of about 300 BC. It is roughly oval in plan, set north to south on a gravel plateau with a particularly deep-cut ditch on the east side. Stout ramparts block the northern approaches and outworks lie on the southern side. The hilltop rises to over 700 feet and has views across the Marshwood Vale.

These greensand gravels and chert were formerly quarried in the north east corner of the fort in an area now largley covered with long grass, foxgloves and scrub. Deciduous woodland is developing in the eastern ditch and a conifer plantation abuts the north-west side. On the west and the east the promontory falls away steeply.

Coney's Castle, and a total of 86 acres, was bought by the National Trust in 1975 with a legacy from Mrs. (Katharine) Olive Pass, widow of Douglas Pass. As for its name, the antiquary Charles Warne suggested in 1872 that "Coney" derived from "Cyning," a Saxon king. This is implausible, the obvious explanation being that coneys were rabbits. Norman warreners who introduced the animals to this country utilised promontories and existing enclosures, like this, to minimise the chances of escape.

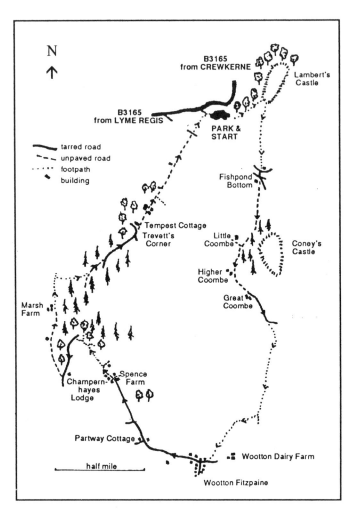

N ↑

B3165
from CREWKERNE

Lambert's
Castle

B3165
from LYME REGIS

PARK &
START

— tarred road
– – unpaved road
····· footpath
◆ building

Fishpond
Bottom

Tempest Cottage
Trevett's
Corner

Little
Coombe

Coney's
Castle

Higher
Coombe

Marsh
Farm

Great
Coombe

Spence
Farm

Champern-
hayes
Lodge

Partway Cottage

half mile

Wootton Dairy Farm

Wootton Fitzpaine

● The six mile walk begins from the National Trust car park at Lambert's Castle, midway between Lyme Regis and Crewkerne. Near the summit of the hill, just above the tree line, there is a track on the south side of the B3165 (with National Trust sign set back from the roadside) which leads to a parking area (Ordnance Survey map reference SY 376 988). This track is two hundred and fifty yards east of a junction with a road sign to "FISHPOND".

• Walk straight ahead from the car park, through a gate into a field; this used to be the racecourse. A beech wood is to your left. Follow the fence which brings you to the ditch and bank of Lambert's Castle. Here turn around and leave the fort by the entrance in the middle of the plateau, 50 yards from the trees. You are now heading just left of centre along the spur of the hilltop into an area of birch scrub and bracken. As you descend you face the sea. In the near distance is the closest of the 160-feet electricity pylons.

• At the foot of the stony track there is a complex double set of road junctions. Cross the first tarred road and walk down to the bottom of the triangular junction in 30 paces. Then in another 20 paces you come to the crossroads at Peter's Gore. Here you continue straight ahead, but not up the tarred road. To the right of it, on the level and in the angle between the roads to "WOOTTON FITZPAINE" and "FISHPOND" there is a bridleway. This farm track passes Gipsies End, goes under the pylon line and takes you straight to the conifer-clad foothills of Coney's Castle.

• I am asking the National Trust to provide a path up through the trees to the earthworks, but there is no restriction upon you trying to find your own. This is buzzard country; you'll frequently see these great birds coming out of the upper tree canopy, or circling and soaring above the valley fields. Theirs is the mewing call that haunts these hills.

• The bridleway skirts the valley farms of Little Coombe, Higher Coombe and Great Coombe. Keep going straight ahead and avoid the tracks that turn towards the farms. Beside the third, the bridleway becomes a concrete road which takes you up the slope. The next section is tarred. On the bend, in 150 yards, you come to a stile in the right hand fence. Cross the stile and keep walking straight ahead. A public path goes around the head of the coombe to a stile in the holly hedge on the other side.

• Walk straight ahead across this arable field aiming for Charmouth church tower at the bottom of the 'V' of the sea. After the gate go right of centre, across the next pasture then forty yards up from the far corner of the field turn right through a gate. You are now looking inland, westwards across the valley, and walk over to the gate facing you on the other side of this field. Follow the left hand hedgerow and on rounding the corner you come to an iron gate. Walk right of centre across this field, down to the village of Wootton Fitzpaine.

● Turn right at the lane, cross the bridge, and walk half a mile uphill towards "MONKTON WYLD, FISHPOND" Keep straight on for "LAMBERT'S CASTLE" at the next junction (but beware of revolving road signs) and pass Partway Cottage. Then in one hundred and fifty yards you come to another junction. Here you ignore the "FISHPONDS" sign (with an added 's') and keep going straight on, up the hill, "To Spence Farm Only." Keep walking straight ahead at the farm following the telegraph poles through the farmyard, but stop immediately after going round the corner. You are faced with two gates; left into a field and right to a cottage. Take the left option where a public footpath enters the field and follows the left-hand hedgerow.

● At the end of the field cross the fence bars into the bluebell and beech tree fringes of what is otherwise a spruce plantation. In twenty paces you turn left, along the main woodland path, and then fork left between two red posts.

This second track brings you to the tarred road in another fifty yards. Turn left along the road, downhill to the end of the wood in a quarter of a mile.

● Turn right opposite Champernhayes Lodge bungalow, along the track to Marsh Farm. After this second cluster of buildings, in half a mile, the bridleway becomes a double-hedged green lane. In two hundred yards it turns sharply to the right and climbs into the conifers.

● Turn left along the main forest road which brings you up to the tarred road. Turn left along this lane to Trevitt's Corner in three hundred yards. Turn left at the first junction, following the "Hawkchurch" sign, but then continue straight ahead in thirty paces. Walk uphill, along the stony track past Tempest Cottage, about which I speculated earlier.

● In a mile the bridleway brings you back on to the greensand plateau at Lambert's Castle Hill. Cross the tarred road and walk straight ahead along the grassy path on the other side. To the left is the precious patch of purple moor grass.

● The path brings you to another stony track, turn right along it and return to your car.

Stonebarrow Hill & Golden Cap

Paths across the National Trust's spectacular Golden Cap Estate on Dorset's western seaboard are being revamped because so many of them have literally fallen over the cliff. Landslips are a continuing geological process that has now eaten away most of the legally "definitive" line of the coast path. The situation is positively dangerous for those who ignore the mud-slides and insist on using two public footpaths that lead down to what can look like a deceptively inviting beach.

Two people drowned when they failed to find the path back up the slippery slope. These are still shown on Ordnance Survey maps even though they have ceased to exist on the ground — disappearing with stiles, steps and even a coastal radar station which slid off the edge of Cain's Folly in the middle of the war.

Constructively, as well as removing treacherous and non-existent paths from the official map, the National Trust is providing an additional four miles of public bridleways and an extra mile of public footpaths. Even after they win legal validity it is going to take years before they filter through to Ordnance maps — and the landslips are in motion again following winter rains.

Just in case this puts you off country walking for life, it should be emphasised that this five mile walk is a departure from our otherwise rigid rule of sticking to public rights of way. In places it will stray from the legal line in order to keep you safe, and use some of the new network or replacement paths that the National Trust has created.

It also keeps clear of the proposed and controversial rerouting of the A35 trunk road — as a dual carriageway that will slice through the estate — which the Trust intends fighting all the way to Parliament.

Such a lot of hassle surrounds this tranquil landscape which is a glorious mix of wild and dramatic coastline and traditionally farmed small pastures with dense hedgerows. Above the sandy cliffs, cross-sectioned by the sea at Golden Cap itself, are the chert-topped plateaus of Stonebarrow Hill, Chardown Hill, Hardown Hill, and Langdon Hill.

The first two are on the course of this walk, as well as Golden Cap, with skyline views of the other two. Between them is the lost village of Stanton St Gabriel, now reduced to a farmhouse and a cottage plus a ruined church, which decayed when the coast road was moved inland to Morcombelake in 1825 — another casualty of those landslips.

A contributory factor was that this was a fishing village where kegs of brandy were more important than legitimate catches. As smuggling declined after the Napoleonic wars the community fell on hard times. The last recorded use to which the church was put, whilst still consecrated, was for the hiding of contraband.

Above it rises Golden Cap, the crowning jewel of the south coast — it is higher than Beachy Head — would be acquired in 1978 as an appropriate memorial to the Earl of Antrim, who as National Trust chairman from 1966 had spearheaded the Enterprise Neptune campaign that saved this seven mile length of Lyme Bay from the double threats of caravan camps and intensive agriculture.

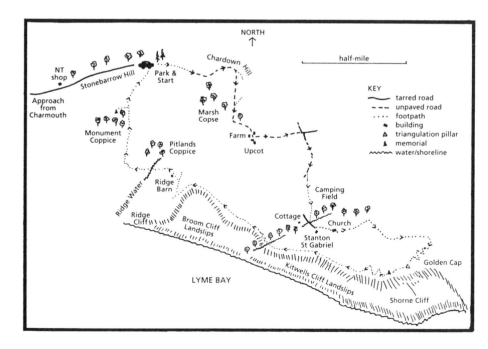

• Enter the estate from the Charmouth end. You turn south from the A35 at the eastern "Charmouth" turn, which is on the Bridport side of the River Char, and pass Newlands caravan camp. You then pass a milestone ("6 to Bridport, 6 to Axminster") and take the left-hand turning on the bend at the eastern end of Charmouth village. The turning, between Newlands House and Seadown House, is signed to "STONEBARROW".

• Climb Stonebarrow Lane. Proceed with caution, as it is steep and narrow, and sound your horn on the first bend. After the beech trees you cross a cattle-grid and enter National Trust land.

• Drive across the high plateau of Stonebarrow Hill to the car-park at the far end. This is beyond the shop compound (a Cold War radar installation) and is half a mile from the cattle-grid. You park and start beside a pine clump (Ordnance Survey map reference SY 399 925).

• Walk towards the trees and fork right, along the seaward option to "ST GABRIELS, GOLDEN CAP". Head down the hillside, towards the great coastal headland and thatched farmhouse at its foot.

• What becomes a farm road then skirts the side of the bowl in the south-facing slope of Chardown Hill. After following it around the corner of the hill, climbing gradually, you pass a bridleway turning to your left. Continue straight ahead, down into a hollow, to Upcot Farm.

• Turn left at the junction beside the farmyard, towards "ST GABRIELS". In 400 yards you come to a hillside crossroads.

• Turn right here, seawards, and continue to follow the unpaved road towards the hamlet of St Gabriels. Fork left in 300 yards, through the gate with the camping club notice, and follow the hedgerow straight ahead. Keep it and the camping field to your left.

• Go through the gate at the bottom end of the field and turn right of centre, to rejoin the lane.

• Turn left, cross St Gabriel's Bridge, and walk up the slope to the thatched farmhouse and the former village green. In 1650 there were 23 families living around it.

• Turn left at the house, uphill to "GOLDEN CAP ½" and pass the thirteenth century parish church.

• Then continue straight ahead for 300 yards, following the track

beside the left-hand hedgerow.
- In the next field you turn right towards the 618-feet summit of the highest cliff on the South Coast of England. Turn left to follow the fence at the top end of the field. Our ascent is going to be from the east. Morcombelake and Hardown Hill are to the left, on the other side of the Morcombelake Bowl — where the results of the A35 bypass will look their most horrendous.
- As you enter the next field you are looking towards the Chesil Beach and Portland. Now turn right, into the upper corner, and begin the real climb. From here the only way is up.
- The triangulation pillar at the top of the steps is followed by the memorial stone to Lord Antrim, who died in 1977 (note the matrix or cast of an ammonite in the rear of the boulder). The low mounds form a line of prehistoric cairns.
- Next comes the zig-zag descent towards "CHARMOUTH 3". Lyme Regis is ahead and Lyme Bay to your left. Follow the coast path for a mile.
- This runs along the top of the undercliff, above active mud-slides along Kitwells Cliff. The path then drops into the lower end of the valley, to a footbridge that crosses St Gabriel's Water.
- Climb the winding flight of steps up the other side. Then follow the path in an inland loop around the outer edge of the overgrown, and hopefully less active, Broom Cliff landslips. Look out for foxes and green woodpeckers.
- Half a mile after the footbridge you cross the seaward fence-bars, to the left of a gate, into the field above Ridge Cliff. You now have what can be a magical view of Lyme Regis and its Cobb harbour.
- Turn right immediately on the other side of the hedge and cross into the next field, heading towards "STONEBARROW HILL, MORCOMBELAKE".
- Then turn left beside the gate — the one you saw from the other side — and pass to the right of Ridge Barn. In the next field you follow the left-hand hedgerow down to Ridge Water.
- Cross the bridge and fork left. Then follow the hedgerow ahead and uphill, keeping it on your right, almost into the top corner of the adjoining field, and enter the following one.
- Now turn right, inland and keep the dense hedgerow to your right.

In the next field you continue straight ahead, up the dip, towards gorse-covered hillside. This is Stonebarrow Hill.

● As you climb, Monument Coppice is to your left. A path leads into its top side. There is a memorial, an obelisk seven feet high, behind railings near the upper corner:

"THIS STONE MARKS THE SPOT WHERE ROBERT HENRY HILDYARD ESQUIRE FELL DEAD WHILST OUT SHOOTING, SEPTEMBER 16th 1876, AGED 40. HE WAS 2nd SECRETARY IN H.M. DIPLOMATIC SERVICE. LORD OF THE MANOR OF CATHERSTON AND J.P. FOR THE COUNTY. HE WAS THE ONLY CHILD OF HIS MOTHER AND SHE WAS A WIDOW ....

"LET THOSE WHO VISIT THIS SPOT SAY FROM THEIR HEARTS, MAKE HIM TO BE NUMBERED WITH THY SAINTS IN GLORY EVERLASTING."

● Carry on uphill to the gate and enter the hillside. Fork right and climb to the top, to the skyline pines and your car.

Lyme Regis from the landslipped Charmouth Road

Golden Cap
& Seatown

Dorset has the highest cliff on the south coast of England. In excess of Beachy Head, though not as convenient for driving off, its plateau stands at 618 feet above the adjacent sea level, between the valleys of Stanton St Gabriel and Seatown on the shore of Lyme Bay. It is a distinctive cliff with a colourful name that perfectly captures its appearance as the broad band of sand catches the sun. The flat top is a horizontal mass of chert. Below is the yellow of fine sand, foxmould, which is upper greensand of the Lower Cretaceous period. This contrasts with the underlying dark clays.

An extensive seascape is visible from the top, from Start Point around to Portland Bill, and there is a breath-taking view down to the inshore waters. Landslipped debris and mud-slides have carried a ribbon of rocks into the sea. They are known, from east to west, as The Corner, Cann Harbour, The Cove and the Western Patches. It is classic landform geology.

Twenty-six acres of the top part, surrounded by foothills already owned by the National Trust, were bought for the nation in 1978 as a memorial to Lord Antrim. This is commemorated by a large block of Purbeck stone which was brought to the summit in the scoop of a bulldozer. An inset slate inscription records: "Golden Cap. Given by members of the National Trust in memory of the Earl of Antrim KBE, chairman of the National Trust from 1966 until his death in 1977."

On the other side, prominent in the upper seaward corner, is part of the matrix of a big ammonite. This is particularly apposite, for the ashes of Bradford Abbas geologist Sidney Savory Buckman were scattered from Golden Cap in 1929. His pioneering work with ammonites from the quarries around Sherborne showed how they could be used to date the rocks from which they had been taken. Many others have been scattered here. The oldest known burials, beneath two cairns which stand about four feet high, probably date from about 1600BC in the Bronze Age.

Below Golden Cap is a remarkable seaside valley characterised by small fields and overgrown hedgerows of a nineteenth century mixed farming landscape that has been preserved by the National Trust. These are lush herb-rich meadows on a clay soil. Nowhere else in Dorset is unimproved pastureland still farmed on this scale. There are also coppices and larger woods fringing the spring-line and in places stretching across the valley floor.

No service has been held in the thirteenth century lias-stone ruin of St Gabriel's church since before 1800. It still stands, as a roofless shell in its own parish as a reminder that the nearby thatched cottage and farmhouse used to be part of a dense cluster of buildings. In 1650 there were twenty families living around the green. After the French wars the church was "frequently used as a receiving house for smuggled kegs of brandy." The porch and walls of the rectangular single-cell church were capped and restored to their present reasonably impressive state, after years of neglect, following acquisition by the National Trust in 1967.

Rev. C. V. Goddard, he vicar of Chideock in the 1890s, recorded smuggling tales from Seatown. Rev. T. Worthington, a curate at Chideock in 1880, also wrote of the scale of the local free-trading: "Within the memory of some of the inhabitants there used to be from thirty to forty fishermen at Seatown, ostensibly employed in their lawful avocations, but really in smuggling. Not the fishermen only, but as in other seaside places half a century ago, the inhabitants in general were implicated in this contraband traffic, of which the sin, in their eyes, consisted only in being found out. Numerous stories are told of their hair-breadth escapes from the clutches of the excise officers."

Seatown beach also has a place in history as the first landing place for the Duke of Monmouth's rebel army on the morning of 11th June, 1685, when two men were rowed ashore. An English gentleman, Thomas Dare, was accompanied by Andrew, Lord Fletcher, a fiery Scot. The latter was second-in-command of the Duke's cavalry and they slipped into Dorset as the advanced party to organise the imminent attempt at seizing the throne for Monmouth from his uncle, James II. Their exploits charted a course for failure that would be consistent with that for the expedition as a whole. Fletcher pulled rank to commandeer Dare's horse. The Englishman refused and raised his whip, at which Fletcher shot him through the head. Volunteers who witnessed the incident wanted Fletcher strung up for murder but he was smuggled back aboard ship and escaped to Spain. Nevertheless these were two disastrous own-goals for Monmouth's side. Fletcher would have been invaluable — an aggressive Scot was just what Monmouth lacked at the head of his cavalry for the skirmish at Bridport and the rout at the Battle of Sedgemoor. And Thomas Dare also had a vital position, as the paymaster for the operation.

Lying outside the beach-side public house, the Anchor Inn, is the fourteen feet long rusty and pebble encrusted anchor of the *Hope* which was a three hundred and fifty ton, thirty gun treasure ship wrecked on the Chesil Beach, opposite Fleet, on the night of 16 January, 1749. The anchor was found seventy five yards off the Chesil Beach by West Bay fisherman Jack Woolmington in September 1986, and sold to publican David Miles.

Returning up-channel to her home port of Amsterdam, having been trading or more likely engaging in piracy in the West Indies, the *Hope* was washed ashore in "tempestuous weather". The mast snapped and crashed on the beach enabling the captain, Boii Cornelizs, and his 73 hands to clamber to safety on the pebbles. "Ship ashore" was the cry that spread at day break through Portland, Weymouth and the villages. Her cargo, mostly in gold, was worth £50,000 - a fortune in the then value of money - and was plundered by "a vast concourse" who pillaged the vessel "as soon as the reflux of the sea had made the ship accessible." They roughly pushed the crew aside and disregarded their faltering foreign accents: "No wreck. The goods ours. Bring it to we and we will pay for it." By this they meant salvage money but the hostile croud grew to an estimated four thousand people who held the Chesil Beach for several days. They were organised by Augustin Elliott, a Portland labourer, who "was the muster-master, the treasurer and divider of the prey amongst his plundering regiment." They were eventually brought to a halt by three justices of the peace and an armed party which went on to carry out house-to-house searches and recovered £25,000 for agents of the ship's owners. Elliott was put on trial at Dorchester on 15 July 1749 but acquitted by a sympathetic jury after a six hour hearing.

At Seatown, the former coastguard service building, the Watch House became the holiday home of Huyshe Wolcott Yeatman-Biggs who was enthroned as fifty-fifth Bishop of Coventry in 1918. His memorial, acclaimed as the finest bronze effigy of a bishop since the Renaissance, was badly damaged during the blitz.

This is a comparatively short walk of five miles, but it inevitably involves some effort as you go from sea-level to the top of Golden Cap. That ascent is stretched over a mile of hill-climb with the steepest bit coming at the end.

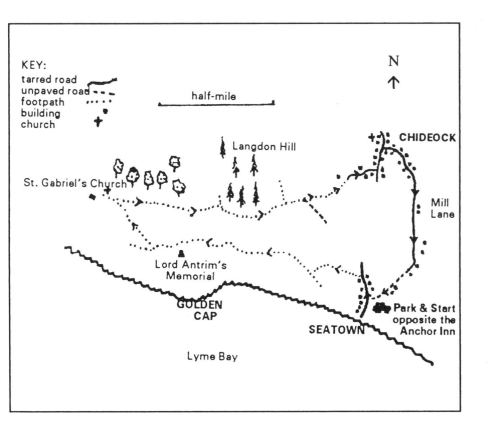

• Turn south from the A35 at Chideock, turning off the main street in the middle of the village, into Seahill Lane which is signposted to "Seatown". In a mile you come to the sea and park on the left, opposite the Anchor Inn (Ordnance Survey map reference SY 420 917). Spot the big anchor lying outside from the wreck of the *Hope* of Amsterdam.

• Turn right along this lane, uphill and away from both the sea and the Anchor. Go round the corner and pass Glenacres. Thirty yards after the house turn left, through a gap in the stone wall. This path crosses a stile and skirts the grounds of Glenacres to bring you into a field.

• Walk straight ahead across this arable field to the stile beside the little beech and pine wood on the other side. You are heading towards the summit of the Golden Cap. After the footbridge the only way is up, via fencing bars and a hunting gate. Turn right on reaching the main cliff path and keep walking uphill. Proceed to the top of Golden Cap (shunning the easier options that are signed inland!).

• You pass the memorial to National Trust chairman The Earl of Antrim in whose memory the headland was bought after his death in 1977. Make sure that you admire the ammonite cast in the back of his Purbeck boulder.

• Here on the only way is down, in the direction of "CHARMOUTH 3" and Lyme Regis. On entering the first field turn right and then head left of centre, inland to the bottom corner of the field and the ruins of St Gabriel's church. Turn right and follow the dense hedge, keeping to the same field and with your back to the chapel, to walk uphill and above St Gabriel's wood.

• On entering the next field ensure that you are heading right of centre towards the right hand end of the skyline conifer plantation on the Langdon Hill plateau. From the top part of this herb-rich pasture you cross into the next field. Head for the right hand end of Langdon Wood. Follow the "SEATOWN, CHIDEOCK" path, beside the lower salt-spray suffering pines. This becomes a dirt track which is Pettycrate Lane.

• Keep walking downhill but make sure that you fork left half a mile away from the wood, off the main track which has become Combrey Lane. Your path narrows and dips down into Chideock and you are walking towards the contorted skyline of Quarry Hill. This track can be muddy at all times of the year. The lower section is tarred and passes St Mary's and Holme Cottage as you approach Seahill Lane. Turn left at the junction, passing Fairways, Ridwood and Yew Cottage. Next are Vine Cottage, Anvil Cottage, Cob Cottage and Barncroft.

● Turn right at the thatched cottage on the next corner into Mill Lane which is a hundred yards before the A35. This returns you to the open country after Golden Cap Holiday Park. The concrete road brings you past the Mill and back to Seatown and your car. Note the packhorse bridge to your left as the cars come into sight. It is neatly cobbled, from its restoration by the Manpower Services Commission for the National Trust in 1984.

Golden Cap Estate

Thorncombe Beacon & Eype Down

Though one of the greatest cliffs of the English Channel, it has been the fate of Thorncombe Beacon to be dwarfed in the public mind by its more conspicuous neighbour, Golden Cap. They stand two miles apart as equal partners in the extent and breadth of their seaward views, from Start Point to Portland Bill, but it could be argued that Thorncombe Beacon is much the more interesting because it has Golden Cap as part of its view.

Unarguably, its inland vista is much superior. There are fewer tree-covered minor hills to block Thorncombe's panorama of Chideock's valley opening out into the lush green landscape of the Marshwood Vale.

Historically it is the 508-feet Thorncombe Beacon that has the claims to fame and indeed flame. Prehistory is represented by three Bronze Age burial mounds, one of these round barrows being of a size worthy of a warrior chieftain.

It was Thorncombe Beacon, rather than Golden Cap, that had the warning lights in Armada and Napoleonic invasion times. It was the crucial link between Abbotsbury and the Devon coast, though one of the weakest of the chain in that this seaboard is notorious for the instant onset of sea-fret when the clouds drop to 300 feet.

In 1940 came the warning system that could penetrate the mists, see in the dark, and bend over the horizon. Radar was operational along this coast both for the skies, from the Battle of Britain onwards, and in countering the hit-and-run tactics of E-boats, which were a lethal threat for the duration — the war in the Channel continued until the Battle of Normandy in the summer of 1944. There were several secret installations on the present-day National Trust lands, including one that persisted for 25 years into the Cold War.

Wartime concrete and bricks on Thorncombe Beacon included a large underground bunker set in the mediaeval beacon mound just above the cliff-edge. This is no more. It was blown up by Royal Engineers, at the behest of the National Trust, in the 1970s. Had it survived another decade it would have been listed as an ancient monument for its 50th anniversary.

The Trust was given Thorncombe Beacon and its chert-capped ridge of yellow sands by playwright Robert Cedric Sherriff in 1966. He lived behind the trees on the leeward slope, in the stone-built Down House Farm.

R. C. Sherriff's first performance, in aid of a school chapel fund in 1921, led to a professional career that opened with *Journey's End* being produced at the Savoy Theatre. Films now needed words and he established his reputation as a dramatist with *The Invisible Man* and *Goodbye Mr Chips*. His last epic scriptwriting would be *The Dam Busters* (two words, originally) from Paul Brickhill's narrative of the legendary exploits of Guy Gibson and 617 Squadron.

He never reached quite the same peaks with his novels, but here too the output was substantial — from *The Fortnight in September of 1931* to *The Wells of St Mary's* which was published 30 years later. His autobiography was *No Leading Lady*.

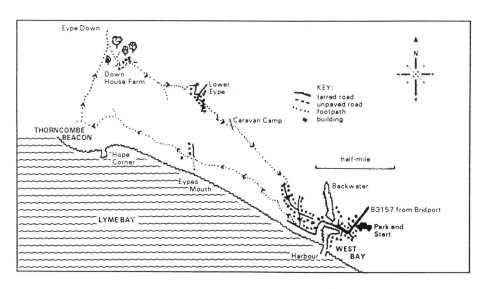

THORNCOMBE BEACON & EYPE DOWN, page 2

The efforts of R. C. Sherriff and now the National Trust have held caravan-country at bay. That has been confined to the valley and lower hills at Eype. Northwards from Down House, Eype Common was successfully registered as common land and is a wilderness of bracken and scrub.

Determined hikers make for Golden Cap, the Everest of these parts, and the Thorncombe Beacon hinterland has been left in semi-solitude. It is within easy walking distance of the heartland of the holiday shore, Bridport Harbour at West Bay and this five mile route stays seaward of the new cut of the A35 that now by-passes the town.

● Park and start at West Bay. There is a large long-stay car-park on the left side as you come into the seaside resort along the main road, the B3157 (Ordnance Survey map reference SY 465 904). It is beside the ivy-clad shell of the Victorian West Bay station which failed to bring the expected flow of visitors and prosperity. The old railway, which ran along the east side of the car-park closed to passengers in 1930 and to goods traffic in 1962. The track back to the town station was lifted in 1965 and a ten year battle then failed to save the remainder of this attractive coastal branch-line.

● So much for the Great Western Railway. You turn left and walk around the fishing boats in the harbour, via the ice-cream and whelk stalls, to the Quayside and Esplanade on the far side.

● At the end of the first section of promenade you climb the cliff steps beside a stone commemorating the 1969 sea defence works. This rather weathered stone was laid by George Mansell who, as chairman of Dorset County Council, declared he wasn't going to have any "roads used mainly as public paths" in the county and struck off a whole category of rights-of-way, leaving disputes that simmer to this day.

● You are heading towards Lyme Regis and come to the holiday hamlet of Eype in a mile, after having skirted an old quarry with half a lime kiln and some terminal slippage on the side facing the ocean. Keep clear of the landform geology in areas where is has decided to change shape. There was no sign of similar troubles on the rest of the walk but things can change and there have been recent problems on the National Trust's Golden Cap estate.

● "Apparently one couple was drowned after trying to follow a land-slipped route in the area of Cain's Folly," regional director David Bett told me. Part of the problem is that maps and walks books can soon be out of date. His advice and mine is that you observe emergency signs and if you find your intended course is crumbling or sinking you should immediately divert inland. That last word is an important one — never go seaward of a cliff-fall or landslide.

● At Eype you cross the stream and walk up through the car-park. Follow the sign "SEATOWN 2 CHARMOUTH 5". Pass to the right of the chalet, upwards on to National Trust land.

● Climb to the summit of the ridge, which is Thorncombe Beacon. It has a 1988 cast-iron fire-holder to celebrate the Armada — which used to be called the Spanish Armada until Spain joined the European Community. The seat is a memorial to Geff Denslow, who died in 1986 and had been the National Trust's assistant warden for the estate since 1976.

● Turn your back on the sea and walk inland, passing a large prehistoric burial mound. A hundred yards to the right of it you cross a stile and follow the top of the ridge towards Eype Down.

● In a quarter of a mile you enter this bracken-smothered common. Climb half-way down the knoll but then turn right, in a hundred yards, and walk downhill. You are now facing Bridport. The path gradually bends to the right and you then turn right, into the sycamores, plus the odd sweet chestnut, that surround R. C. Sherriff's old home, Down House Farm.

● Here you turn left, between the house and the barns, and walk down the main track. Pass the house and Ebb House bungalow. Opposite this, and the entrance to Downlands, you turn right.

● Cross the stile beneath another clump of sycamores. You are heading towards Lower Eype, beneath St Peter's chapel, built in 1865, and the television relay mast.

● As you walk across the field,

following the right-hand hedgerow at first, you aim for a point to the right of the houses. This brings you to a gate in the hedge facing you.

● On the other side you turn left to head for the chapel. Walk down to the hedge and go through the gate, into the valley floor, to the track that leads up to the left and then down to the right, into Lower Eype Farm. You then pass below a thatched cottage and climb up the slope to the village street at Primrose Cottages.

● Turn right and then left, beside Pilgrim's Latch. In 50 yards, at the next corner, you continue straight ahead, opposite Bethlehem, between Barn Cottage and the Olde Barn (conversion).

● Cross the stile and follow the track, beside the hedgerow. Keep following this hedge, leaving the track where it departs through a gate, and cross the valley floor. Follow the hedgerow until just after it kinks to the right, 100 yards down from the caravan camp.

● Here you cross a stile and then turn left, to follow the other side of the hedge up to a stile beside the caravans. Walk straight ahead, between the mobile homes, to the hedge on the far side.

● Turn right along it for a short distance, to find a gate on the north side of a toilet block. Forty yards to the left is a well-hidden wartime pillbox, immersed in the hedge and covered with ivy.

● Cross at the gate, which may be due for replacement with a stile, into the field. Head diagonally across it, downhill in the direction of the sea at West Bay.

● Follow the left-hand hedgerow in the next field and cross a stile which is set in the gate at the end.

● Then walk down between the wooden fences, to the top end of a neat estate of bungalows. This is Brit View Road and you should have emerged beside number 22, which is Horizons.

● Walk down the road and turn right at the junction. You are now in West Bay and all roads lead to the harbour.

Eggardon
& Powerstock Common

The outer lip of Dorset's chalkland massif is explored on this seven mile walk into the deep-cut valleys at the edge of the Marshwood Vale. It is southern English scenery with a relish of western grandeur.

The double gems are the immense prehistoric hill-fort at Eggardon Hill — half of it in National Trust ownership — and the best wild country in Dorset on the slopes of the former Powerstock Common. That this medieval backwater is still a wilderness, now in conservation hands, owned by Dorset Wildlife Trust, is due to the abrasive campaign that was mounted in its defence by author and broadcaster Kenneth Allsop shortly before his death in 1973.

He pulled no punches in denouncing the Forestry Commission for clear-felling proposals that would have reduced this magic bogland of fantastically gnarled oaks festooned with epiphytic growths of lichens, mosses and ferns into yet another spread of conifer monoculture.

Here, and on the adjoining Eggardon Hill, you can sample cherished landscapes that have survived primarily because of the fuss caused by committed journalism.

The price to pay on the ground for lush scenery is that there are damp patches. These are at their worst where the walk crosses the spring-line, principally at Powerstock Common, so dress in the expectation of squelching.

The walk is worth that effort. As we descended upon Castle Mill farmhouse a young motorcyclist approached it from the sensible direction, along a firm track. Power gave way to pedestrians. "It's nice out," he said, dressed in black leathers, to a backdrop of a sky that was just a little lighter.

I agreed and muttered something trite about the landscape being enhanced by its rougher edges and the coolness of the day. "You can't beat it," the young man continued. "I went to Spain once but I don't think I'll go again. Who needs it?"

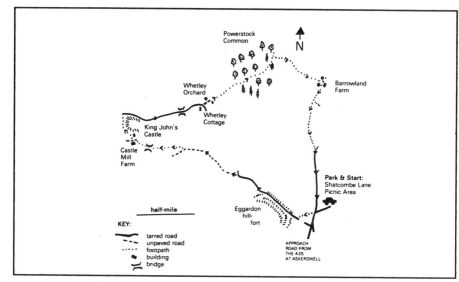

The walk starts from the "Shatcombe Lane Picnic Area" which is a wide area of roadside verge half a mile on the Wynford Eagle side of Eggardon Hill. The spot is on the high downs midway between Bridport and Maiden Newton. Approaching the area on the A35 you turn north at Askerswell, three miles east of Bridport, drop down into this village and then climb the steep hill beneath the pylon lines. At the summit a lane joins from the right and then you take the next right which is signposted "WYNFORD EAGLE 2½, MAIDEN NEWTON 4½".

Two hundred yards along, on the left side, you come to a series of grassy parking bays which

Dorset County Council has cut from the blackthorn scrub. Turn right on leaving your car, and follow the lane uphill to the junction.

Turn right, which is signposted "TOLLER PORCORUM, MAIDEN NEWTON" (Maiden Newton appears on two of the three pointers) and then in only ten paces you turn left across fence-bars into the field. Walk left of centre across the field to the left-hand end of the great Iron Age hill-fort facing you. My map shows the public path emerging from the corner of the field but there we found a combined barbed wire and electrified fence. The farmer has, however, provided climbable fence bars (with insulated cable) 150 yards left from the corner.

● Turn right along the hilltop lane which becomes a ridgeway literally running along the top of the outer rampart of the 1st century BC fortifications. These are formidable with three waves of banks and ditches which were staggered for slingstone warfare.

● At the foot of the hill you turn left, at a widened passing place just where the road begins to bend to the right. Continue keeping the fence and the bottom of the escarpment to your left. As this great hillside falls away the green lane continues through a gate and descends unfenced through tumbling spring-like pastures. There is a view across the Marshwood Vale to Lyme Bay and Start Point.

● You go through two gates and then descend a steeper slope with a fence to your left and a power cable on telegraph poles to your right. Halfway down this hill the track bends to the left and here you continue straight ahead over a stile.

● This puts you on to a footpath up and over a gorse-covered hillock. On the other side you keep the hedgerow to your right, and cross the bridge of grey Victorian engineering bricks that spans the former Bridport branch railway. At the end of the following field the track descends into a fern and garlic smothered hollow on a terrace that slopes down to the thatched Castle Mill Farm beside the stream.

● Turn right beside the wall of the farm, across the footbridge, and follow the stream past the outbuildings and through the clumps of ornamental rhubarb. You then climb the stony track up the hill, ignoring a path that branches off to your left. Above you in the trees are the earthworks of a Norman motte-and-bailey castle. Locals call it King John's Castle. The track passes a gate with a glimpse of the earthworks and then bends down to a tarred lane.

● Turn right, uphill, and re-cross the old railway in half a mile at Whetley Bridge (strange architectural mix — sheets of cast iron with elaborately carved Pennant sandstone toppings to the corners). In 300 yards you pass Whetley Cottage.

● Twenty paces after this cottage you fork left. A rough track passes

Whetley Orchard. Immediately after this cottage and its garden you go straight ahead through an iron gate, next to a barn-garage.

● Keep straight ahead in the field, with the hedgerow to your left for 200 yards, and then walk straight ahead to the wicket gate facing you on the side of the pasture. It is 50 feet to the left of the right-hand corner.

● Continue straight ahead beside the pine stands and climb into the older oakwood of the Dorset Wildlife Trust reserve (its next generation signs will call it the Dorset Trust for Nature Conservation). The primaeval woodland of Powerstock Common supports buzzards, fallow deer, and 37 species of butterflies which have been recorded on the open areas of unimproved herb-rich grassland. Follow the path towards the summit, following the deer-slots among the horse-prints. The top ground, to your right, is bracken covered above the spruce-line. The path gradually rises into an area of older scrub, at the top, and here you follow the main track to the right and come to a wicket gate.

● Leave the reserve and walk into the field. Go straight ahead, down across the valley, to the buildings at Barrowland Farm. Midway, there is a leftward diversion around the slurry below the farm track. At the farm you pass between the barns and then turn right, keeping the farmhouse to your left.

● Keep straight ahead along the farm track until it bends uphill to the left. Here you go through the gate into the field and keep the right-hand fence line immediately to your right. This then becomes an old hedgerow which curves up the hillside. You may find you have to slip under or over the wire to follow the final length of scrubby trees on to the summit.

● Here you are looking across to the earthworks of Eggardon hill-fort strung along the skyline. You then turn left, however, and keep the hill-fort to your right as you cross the arable field to the tarred road.

● Turn right along it, uphill, for half a mile to the junction with the "EGGARDON HILL" roundel on top of the signpost. Turn left, along the lane signposted to "WYNFORD EAGLE". In a short distance this becomes the Shatcombe Lane Picnic Area.

Swyre &
Puncknowle

Only around Abbotsbury does the Dorset coast embark upon an orderly cliffless transition from a wide beach through reed beds and flat meadows into a smooth green hill. Not that more normal aspects of the Dorset seaboard — the tough cliffs of the far west — are ever long out of view. Nor is there any lack of wild places and vast patches of dense scrub give refuge to the plentiful herds of roe deer.

Everywhere there is history, and this five mile walk has short diversions that explore four major monuments which are beside or just off the route. Two are churches, at Swyre and Puncknowle, and the others a lookout from smuggling days and a perfectly preserved limekiln. This century has added the bungalows, though as John Betjeman remarked about Cornwall they have not yet started building them on the sea.

It is easy walking country, though there are two or three arable fields to muddy your feet, and the only proviso is to remember that the coastal meadows may still flood in the wettest winter weeks. Do it on a weekday and you are likely to have company in the sky. My companions were a Lynx and a Sea King.

The walk starts from the B3157 coast road, the one from Bridport to Weymouth, on the hills midway between Burton Bradstock and Abbotsbury.

● Park and start in the hillside layby on the south side of the B3157 just about a mile east of the Bull Inn, Swyre — that is, on the Abbotsbury side of Swyre. It is a hundred yards east from the eastern of two white painted bungalows. The layby is on National Trust land at the edge of Limekiln Hill and has a wooden footpath sign "HARDY MONUMENT 5 — WEST BEXINGTON ½". If you come from the other way, the spot is three miles west of Abbotsbury and you see it as the eastern bungalow and its back extension come clearly into view — it is the

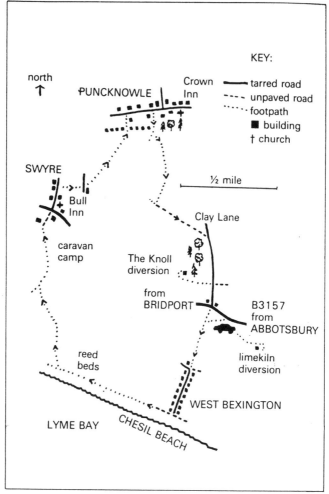

KEY:
- —— tarred road
- --- unpaved road
- ⋯ footpath
- ■ building
- † church

north ↑

PUNCKNOWLE

Crown Inn

½ mile

SWYRE

Bull Inn

Clay Lane

caravan camp

The Knoll diversion

from BRIDPORT

B3157 from ABBOTSBURY

reed beds

limekiln diversion

WEST BEXINGTON

LYME BAY

CHESIL BEACH

first roadside building since you left Abbotsbury. Overshoot and you'll spot a large white signboard for "The Manor Hotel".

● From the layby you take the Bexington option, downhill in a westerly direction. I did it uncharacteristically early in the morning, into the tail of an Atlantic gale, and had pinpoint clarity across to the white cliffs of Beer; the last chalk between England and America. You are also facing Lyme Regis and Charmouth, which is just glimpsed behind Golden Cap — the highest cliff on the South Coast. The grassy path passes between dense scrub, with much blackthorn and wayfaring tree, and joins another track in a hundred yards.

• Turn left here, downhill, following another "WEST BEXINGTON ½" sign. You are now walking straight towards the Chesil Beach. The impenetrable thicket continues all the way on the left side but to the west you have open views across Lyme Bay.

• Near the bottom you come into a cluster of farmyard buildings and continue straight ahead beside the barns, as pointed out by the sign "TO COAST PATH". There are figs around the door of Adam Simon, woodworker. Next you pass the Manor Hotel with its new-old glasshouse provided by Classical Conservatories of St Clements Road, Parkstone. You would only know it was that recent if you had watched it being erected in the autumn winds. (At this point a man pulled up in a red car. "Hullo squire, what are you doing," he inquired, in a manner in which the modern idiom would describe as 'heavy'. "Writing .... that's not the way to ask," I replied. He drove off. It is nice to know the power of the pen is still feared.) You then pass through bungalow land for the final third of a mile to the sea. At the bottom there is a beach-side car-park and a Dorset Heritage Coast information display.

• Turn right and pass the panels, which show the path you are now taking — westward through the West Bexington nature reserve of the Dorset Wildlife Trust. Other panels depict the almost all-weather denizens of the shingle, the species Angler Beach-caster: "Catches include cod, whiting, and rays in the winter; mackerel, bass and flat-fish in the summer. A passing shoal of mackerel can occasionally be seen causing the sea to 'boil'." In the nature reserve you come to clumps of thrift which mingle with the white sea campion and bright-yellow horned poppies. The patches of bluish-green crickled cabbage are sea kale. Wild carrot, with flat creamy flower heads, is another ancestor of our cultivated vegetables. The real rarity is the sea pea. This track is usually submerged by the beach, which is here comprised of a few half inch oval pebbles mixed with plenty of sultana-shaped pea gravel. The reed bed in the mere on the right is also part of the nature reserve.

• At the end of the reed bed, nearly half a mile from the information display, you turn right over a wooden footbridge. Then cross the stile into the field and follow the hedge, which has been dwarfed by salt-wind exposure, towards the valley. You'll spot a caravan camp near the top. It is a mile walk up the valley, keeping the tiny overgrown stream to your right. At the end of the long arable field you come to a clearing beneath a field maple and some young ash trees. Turn right here, following the "SWYRE ½" option over the stile beside a galvanised hunting gate. You are now on pasture land and still keep the thick hedge and then the caravans to your right. There's a neat stone and slate house at the top of this next field. Here I have a chat with a lady, also the wrong side of forty, who has just carried two armfuls of driftwood all the way up from the beach. I feel doubly reassured — human endeavour still exists, and the natives can be friendly.

● Go through the gate and up the short double-hedged track to the main road. Cross over to the church. The village is Swyre and the church is Holy Trinity, which was restored about 1830 and has only one major monument. This is a massive tablet to James Napier,

erected in 1692, which is a wordy biography of the family's descent from "ye ancient family of Lenox in Scotland". There are several railed tombs in the churchyard and a more recent stone which poignantly records John Castle's entry in the annals of the British Empire: "P.o.W. Singapore, February 1941-October 1945."

● Turn right on leaving the churchyard and pass Manor Farm and the willow planted by the Women's Institute in 1974. Opposite is the Old School. Twenty feet after the post-box you turn right.

● Cross the stone and wooden stiles and walk across the field to the similar stiles on the opposite side, just left of the cottage. Then cross the drive to the wooden stile beside the left wall of the cottage. There is a right of way leftward across this arable field but it may be easier to follow the left-hand hedgerow until you reach the small barn after the fourth bungalow from the left. Here there is a stile and you pass "The Cottage" which was the village's Wesleyan Chapel, built in 1849.

● Turn right at the village street and walk down beside Greystones Farm. This is Puncknowle, or

"Punnel" as the locals call it. Continue along the street to the Crown Inn, opposite which is the parish church of St Mary. Take off your shoes! The pyramid-shaped tower is superb. Ditto the Norman font-base with a head and other carvings which is said to have come from St Giles's church, Bexington, which was destroyed by the French — along with the rest of that village — in 1440. It was owned by Bindon Abbey which decided to abandon the coastal community. The Bexington Aisle here at Punnel was built as its memorial, and rebuilt in its present form in 1660. It has a beautiful medieval brass of a praying knight, William Napier. There are Napier monuments all around, including that of Sir Robert Napier, with his epitaph of 1700. His initials, or those of his father, appear in the nail-studs of the seventeenth century door. Its original lock is still in use. Outside, make sure you admire the perfection of Punnel Manor from the wall behind the church, and that you find the fifteenth century octagonal cross — it is a rarity for these to survive intact. It used to stand about where the telephone kiosk (still a K6, Giles Gilbert Scott design, of the 1930s) is now.

● Walk back down to the lych-gate, facing Durban Cottage, and turn left along the street. Retread your paces, about a hundred of them, to West Hay bungalow opposite the Greystones barn.
● Turn left here, along a leafy track signposted: "FOOTPATH TO KNACKERS HOLE OPEN SPACE & CLAY LANE." About fifty feet before the field there is an alternative path to the left which brings you to a wicket gate. This leads you into a wide droveway which ascends the hill. You can look back on Shipton Hill, looking like a capsized boat, and the distant hilltops surrounding the Marshwood Vale.
● Further up the slope you cross a wooden stile and then a stone stile, beside a metal gate. From these you follow the left-hand hedge for a hundred feet, passing another metal gate, and take the track on the left that leads away from a cow-stall.
● This is signposted: "TO CLAY LANE". It is a gravel road that brings you to a tarred road. Turn right along it. At the top of the hill, beside the end of the wood, there is a stone sign on the right: "FOOTPATH TO KNOLL ONLY. NO THROUGH PATH."

It is a worthwhile quarter of a mile diversion up to a romantic windswept sea-mark at 593 feet. This summer house, according to the books, or smugglers' lookout as the villagers assert, has a single tiny room with a fireplace on the landward side. Seaward there are two window seats. Above there is a bedroom, with a blocked fireplace and a single window that looks out over the Chesil Beach. It is a stone roofed building perched on a stone plinth and a four foot high Bronze Age burial mound that has been re-cut into a square. Note as you turn to go back, away from the reservoir, that there is an hexagonal brick and concrete 1940 pillbox concealed in the side of the hill. It makes me believe in the smugglers; once a lookout, always a lookout.

● On returning to the lane, you turn right. You come to the coast road between the bungalows. Though your car is visible to the left it is far safer to cross straight over to the grass track on the other side.

● In a hundred yards it will bring you to a second grass track (signposted: "HARDY MONUMENT") which takes you back to your car without any close encounters with those that are not stationary. Even here there is an opportunity for a further short diversion. If you go into the field and follow the edge of the escarpment for two hundred yards you will come to what is probably the best preserved limekiln in Dorset. Indeed it has given its name to the map — Limekiln Hill. Restoration has been carried out in recent times for the National Trust and you can visualise it in use. It would have been filled from the top with layers of limestone or chalk alternating with wood or coal and slow combustion was necessary to convert the rock into quicklime. Until the 1920s this was the process by which building mortar, limewash and soil dressings were produced — in locations that were as close as possible to the source of supply and the place of intended use. In only a few decades most of these relics of self-sufficiency have been swept away and now very few remain to be cherished as specimens of industrial archaeology.

Old Harry Rocks & Studland

Fifteen years after acquisition by the National Trust, the coastal chalklands of Ballard Down and Old Harry Rocks have been transformed from a reluctant prairie into recovering grassland. Their exposed position has ravaged hopes of full-scale cereal production. Nature is beginning to reassert herself and, though the full flora will take years to recover and perform again, improvements are visible everywhere across several hundred acres that have been rescued by the Trust from the Agricultural Revolution of the 1960s.

Commendably, through land agent Mark Harold, the National Trust has put the clock back to self-sufficient farming of the traditional sort. Permanent grass has been mixed with arable, cows with crops and measures taken to save Manor Farm at Studland from sinking into its own pool of slurry.

This five mile walk is a circuit of Ballard Down and Studland Manor Farm, bringing in the famous off-shore chalk stacks at the Pinnacle, Turf-Rick Rock and the great Old Harry collection that were, until recent times, the only pieces of land in these parts that the plough failed to reach.

An early casualty was the coast path, reduced in parts to virtually single-file width, but it has already widened into something of its former self as a swathe of well-trodden grass. Elsewhere, at the edges of the newly restored turf, there are clusters of tree tubes that will become plantations to supplement the decaying copses at Studland Wood and Warren Wood.

Overcoming problems with the landscape is proving easier than managing those of customer demand. Therefore, in an attempt to cheat the congestion at the heart of the holiday coast, this walk avoids the over-crowded and over-charged car parks of Studland and starts instead from the free and open space of an ordinary back-of-town layby on the northern outskirts of Swanage. Here, in the Ulwell Gap between two ridges of the Purbeck Hill, the scenery is superb with unploughable escarpments which are also mostly National Trust owned.

The route brings in a surfeit of history with the usual Dorset offering of prehistoric monuments being embellished by a bizarre collection of monumental bits of old London reassembled on these hills in celebration of the tapping of pure water from the chalk formation — which enabled the evolution of Swanage from a quarry port into an Edwardian spa.

In more recent times the local quarrying skills have revived Studland's Saxon village cross and given it a new shaft that is a masterpiece of traditional style with a modern theme. Around these lanes, ex-guardsman Christopher Rone was the archetypal village bobby and was spotted by Enid Blyton who invariably spent her holidays in Swanage. She immortalised him as PC Plod in the Noddy stories.

Another literary aside is that the ashes of the novelist and futurist H.G. Wells were scattered in the sea off Old Harry Rocks in 1946 in response to a passage from his work that had been read at the memorial service: "We are all things that make the pass, striving upon a hidden mission, out to the open sea."

On land, you can venture a short distance down the lane beside Studland cross and find St Nicholas Church the oldest intact building in Dorset plus an overdose of memorials to interesting people and events.

Cornet Bankes, of the landowning family, was posthumously awarded the Victoria Cross for cheerfully accepting certain death in lighting the fuse that ended the siege of Lucknow in the Indian Mutiny. A military survivor with an international war record from South America and Spain and Waterloo was Sergeant William Lawrence who ended his days as landlord in the Bankes Arms. His gravestone is so wordy that it qualifies as a biography.

More poignant are the tragic inscriptions to the victims of shipwreck and weekend sailing misadventures in Studland Bay.

As for the church, of reddish brown gritty heathstone, it is notable as "one of only a dozen or so near-complete Norman village churches in England," to quote Fred Pitfield in *Purbeck Parish Churches*.

"Moreover the Norman work is built around the core of a still earlier pre-conquest structure, so that it can be regarded as the oldest surviving complete church in Dorset." In other words the shell is Saxon and — as Dorset has no intact castle or house earlier than fourteenth century Woodsford Castle — it is therefore the oldest complete building in the county.

So this is a walk with superlative history to match the breathtaking scenery.

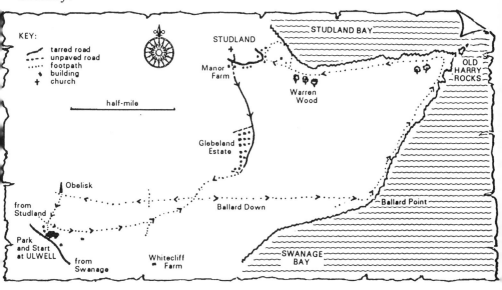

● Park at Ulwell, on the east side of the road just south of Godlingston Hill, in the large lay-by between Swanage Reservoir and Shepherds Farm (Ordnance Survey map reference SZ 021 809). There is a "Welcome to Swanage" sign set in a stone plinth.

● The walk starts at a kissing gate on the east side of the lay-by, beside a gate and 15 yards from the Swanage sign. You cross a clear trickle of water and take the main path, uphill and just left of centre. Keep to the left-hand fence line and pass the "S W ACT 1883" inscription on a block of granite in 30 yards.

● This, and the obelisk of a former City of London gas-lamp on the hill-top, commemorate the

Swanage Water Act and the successful abstraction of pure water from the chalk aquifer.

• Seventy yards after the stone, just above the reservoir buildings, you come to a junction of paths with three options being signed on a marker stone.

• Turn right, following the arrow "TO COAST PATH". This takes you through the scrub at the foot of the Ballard Down escarpment. To the right there are glimpses of Swanage.

• In 150 yards you pass above a luxury home and follow the fence, keeping it to your right. There is now a reasonable view of Swanage Bay. At the end of this pasture the path crosses a stile to enter National Trust land at a "BALLARD DOWN" sign. Continue straight ahead, towards the slanting hillside in the distance.

• In 350 yards, above Whitecliff Farm, you come to a hunting gate and a junction of paths. Turn left here, uphill and with your back to Swanage. There is a notice board and then a stone sign pointing to "Studland", followed by a couple of stone seats.

• Near the summit you come to a hunting gate and continue to the main fence-line which is on the brow of the hill in 70 yards. Here the view suddenly widens into a panorama of Poole Harbour, Bournemouth cliffs, Poole Bay and the Isle of Wight.

• Do not go through the gates but instead turn right, following the hilltop seaward along a path signed to "OLD HARRY ROCKS AND COAST PATH". Continue along this path to the clifftop, in two thirds of a mile. You pass a pair of Bronze Age burial mounds, prehistoric cross-dykes and the remains of a wartime coastal radar station.

• The main track passes an Ordnance Survey triangulation pillar, at 383-feet on the cliffs, and then brings you to the coast path.

• Turn left along it, downhill and towards Old Harry Rocks, with the sea to your right.

• In another mile you are on the edge of Studland village. At the garden fence of the first building, with an attractive Victorian Gothic turret at the seaward corner, you continue straight ahead through the gate for the direct path into the village. The alternative is to turn right and enter Studland via the beach huts and sands and then turn left up the South Beach track.

● Either way you emerge on a lane, beside the public toilets. Turn left here, passing thatched cottages numbers 2 and 3, and walk up to the 1976 "Spaceship Earth" cross by Purbeck marbler Treleven Haysom which is set on a Saxon plinth at the junction of the road leading to St Nicholas Church.

● Facing the cross is the Dairy House of Manor Farm. Turn left beside it, along the track between the farmhouse and its outbuildings, which is signed from the crossroads as a "Public Footpath to Ballard Down and Swanage".

● It takes you via the hillside Glebeland Estate in half a mile. Thirty yards after the last house, Summer Hill, you turn left through a gateway beside an electricity pole. "Swanage 1½", the path is signed.

● On top of Ballard Down there is a stone seat inscribed "REST AND BE THANKFULL" *(sic)* and "D J 1852" for brilliant Victorian law-writer David Jardine who adopted Swanage.

● Go through the gate and turn sharp right, following the fence along the ridge of the hill with an expansive view in both directions. Keep going straight ahead.

● In the dip in just over half a mile you come to the commemorative obelisk, set on a Bronze Age burial mound. The original inscription records the fact that the Cornish granite was "taken down from near the Mansion House, London, and re-erected here in 1892". Note the evidence of its intended purpose at the centre of the displaced hexagonal column, once the lower section of the obelisk, viz the gas-pipe. A plaque gives the more recent history, of demolition "in 1941 to avoid its being of assistance to enemy aircraft during the war" and re-erection in 1973 by the Royal Engineers.

● Turn left at the obelisk, over the stile, and head downhill to Ulwell. There is a caravan camp in the middle distance with Swanage Brickworks behind.

● The path follows a fence down the steep slope and you turn left on reaching the yew trees at the bottom. Keep the trees and the reservoir buildings to your right.

● In a hundred yards you are back at the lay-by and your car.

Scotland &
Purbeck's Texas

Drive to Scotland. I've always wanted to start a Dorset walk with those words! For Scotland has long been my favourite historic building and farmstead of the Isle of Purbeck and, indeed, anywhere.

It is a low-ceiling stone-roofed farmhouse on the heath, midway between the Purbeck Hills and the backwaters of Poole Harbour. The walls are especially fine, but second-hand — being blocks of ashlar from the ruins of Corfe Castle.

That bit of recycling took place in 1665, twenty years after the fortress was demolished for losing the Civil War. The seventeenth century credentials and builder's initials, W.W. for William Whefer, are cut in stone above the porch doorway.

This is an otherwise humble corner of the 16,000 acre estate which passed to the National Trust on the death of Ralph Bankes in 1981. Scotland remains in decent obscurity and rusticity, but commendable Trust intervention has saved its decaying thatched barn.

The result is magnificent and, from a distance, discrete. First you spot the commemorative stone, carved in 1990 with the Trust's oak-sprig logo. Then, around the next corner, comes the real surprise.

Looking out over his garden, it could be a larger than life carving of the 75-year-old farmer I met, William White, except it is lacking the beard that matches his name. I am told it features Derek Cartridge, the mason who led the restoration team, carved by sculptor Jonathan Sells of Corfe Castle.

It is brilliant, not only artistically but in terms of the idea and place — positioned just below the eaves — as a striking revival of Dorset's ancient Celtic traditions.

There are many other gems off the beaten track along this seven mile walk. Sharford packhorse bridge and the elegant New Mills sluices are among the best of their kind, and still confined to path-use only.

Wytch Passage is rustic Dorset in the same league as Scotland, with a tin bath hanging beside the door and only the stumps of a landing stage to hint at the fact that this was the market-day ferry terminal for Corfe villagers crossing the water to Poole.

Now, looking across to Hamworthy , it seems no distance at all. In fact it is a deceptive four miles. There has been a catalogue of tragic drownings over the centuries as rare but recurrent tricky conditions in the land locked harbour have swamped a succession of overladen little craft.

These days most of the activity is on land and generated by British Petroleum. Oilmen and their contractors speed along a network of private roads that sweep through the pines of Rempstone Forest. This walk passes well-site X ('X' for exploratory) which started the bonanza and was bang on target for the discovery of the Wytch Farm oilfield in the autumn of 1973.

Petroleum production licence PL 089, then in the hands of the British Gas Council, hit the bull's-eye after the years of fruitless seismic surveys and drilling failures across the county. In the following year there was

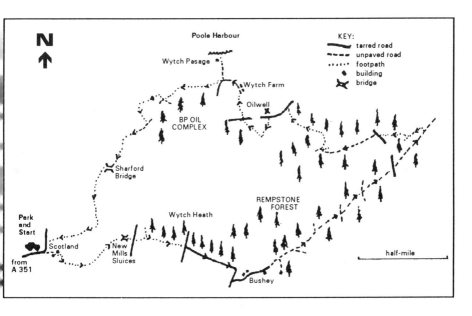

more oil discovered in the Isle of Purbeck than in the whole of Texas.

Extracting from the underground Bridport and Sherwood sands, at 3,000 feet and 5,000 respectively, production has topped 100,000 barrels a year. There are nine billion tonnes in reserve.

This brown gold is the finest quality "British light sulphur-free", and resulted from organic decay in the tropical Jurassic and Triassic ages, between 144 and 248 million years ago.

● Using your own tank of fossil fuel, you take the A351 between Wareham and Corfe Castle. 1.4 miles south of Halfway Inn you turn east at the 'Wytch Farm Oilfield' roundabout.

● Then, in only 50 yards, you turn left along the lane signposted to "SLEPE 1½, ARNE 3". In just under a mile there is a ninety degree left-hand bend with a thatched barn visible straight ahead, 80 yards up a track. This is Scotland (Ordnance Survey map reference SY 961 840).

● There is enough grass verge for one or two cars, by the stile and on the other side of the farm access road. Otherwise continue in search of a suitable patch of grass and walk back to this spot.

● Do not take the stile but walk up the main track to the barn. Turn right beside it and then left at the corner, admiring the carvings. Scotland Farm is to the right.

● After the thatched barn, the path passes between outbuildings, goes through a gate, and turns right, into a paddock.

● Then enter the main field and turn left. Go through the first hedge and then keep the next holly-studded hedge to your left and the view of Corfe Castle to your right.

● Walk the length of the sloping grassland, heading towards a point to the left of the eastern end of the Purbeck Hills. Towards the extremity of the long field you go over the top of the ridge and descend to a central gateway in the hedge facing you, in about 60 yards.

● Turn left of centre in this field and go through a gate in 75 yards. Then turn right of centre and walk across to a stile beside the electricity poles in 100 yards.

● Cross a footbridge and then proceed left of centre to another bridge in 60 yards. These 1711-dated sluices over the Corfe River are all that remains of the extensive New Mills. The west cutwater proclaims the ownership of "WO" and the eastern one is inscribed for "NB".

● On NB's side of the water (for Nathaniel Bankes) you cross a narrow strip of field, left of centre, to a cattle grid, leading on to a road in 40 yards.

● Turn left along it, but only for 15 yards. Then you strike off to the right, crossing the next cattle grid on the other side of the road.

● Follow this track uphill for a hundred yards, to the corner of the pine forest that is called Wytch Heath on the map. Here you proceed straight ahead, keeping the outer line of trees to your left.

● In a quarter of a mile you cross a tarred road at "FIRE RENDEZVOUS POINT ACCESS NO. 3" and continue down the other tarred road opposite. In a quarter of a mile this road bends to the right.

● Then in a hundred yards you come to a junction and turn left. Pass a farmstead and cottage at Bushey. The road then becomes a dirt track, which is Corfe Castle bridleway 8, and you keep going straight ahead along it - ignoring a "PRIVATE ACCESS ONLY" sign, if it is still there. I have complained to Barry Thomas of Dorset County Council's rights-of-way office that it is misleading and therefore unlawful.

● Fifty yards into the fir trees you continue straight ahead, leaving the main track which bends to the right. At the next set of options, in 150 yards, you fork left.

● Then continue straight ahead, uphill, where the track splits again in 50 yards. Ignore other similar offshoots and keep going forward along the main sandy track. It goes gradually uphill, through Rempstone Forest, heading north-east.

● In half a mile you walk over the gentle brow of the ridge and then continue straight ahead at a woodland crossroads.

● In another half mile you cross a tarred road and follow an unmade road on the other side. It is signed to "OWER QUAY". There is also mention of "Vitower". That is the Dorset dialect for what mapmakers spell as 'Fitzworth' and I am delighted that my 1972 call for its revival has got it back into use on the ground.

• Count the telegraph poles. In a quarter of a mile, at pole number 6, you turn left and walk over to the corner tree in 25 yards.

• Turn left here, and then left again in another 25 yards. Follow a straight ride between the pine stands.

• You are now heading west, with your previous course visible through the trees to your left. In 150 yards you turn right at a forest crossroads and drop down to the tarred road at telegraph pole number 47.

• Turn right along the road for 50 yards. Then turn left on to a wide gravel track. The gap in the tree cover to the left is the foresters' grudging acknowledgement of Green Pond bog.

• Next the gravel road bends to the right, after which you come to a junction of tracks in 50 yards. Here the path you want is the one that is right of centre with a clearing of tussock bog to the left, and the usual ubiquitous tree cover to the right.

• You head north for a hundred yards and then bend left to pass under the electricity power line. In a third of a mile you pass the extensive bogs of Wytch Moor, which you keep to your left.

• You come to a gate and stile beside a tarred road. Turn left along this road and cross at the stiles adjacent to the double set of cattle grids.

• To your right is a view across the inlets of Poole Harbour to what was Hamworthy power station. In 200 yards you came, in December 1991, to the rig and cabins of Boldon Drilling. This site was already historic, being the spot where an earlier boring, in 1973, first struck the Wytch Farm oilfield.

• Turn left just before the oil site, at the west end of the causeway, through a gate on to a path that follows the fence along the other side of Wytch Moor. You are now heading south, towards the Purbeck Hills. Squelch to the double supports of the power line and pass between the poles.

• Then follow the pylon line uphill, onto firm ground, with trees to your left and the bog behind you. Now, on a north-westerly course, you return to the oilmen's road at "FIRE RENDEZVOUS POINT No 7".

• Here you turn right for 20 yards and then turn left, through the gate. Keep the hedgerow to your left for 150 yards and then turn left through a gap and immediately right through a gate into a double fenced track leading to the pre-oilwell Wytch Farm which is now well within the sound, sight and smell of its famous successor.

● Pass beside the farm and its barns, keeping to the left of the buildings, along a track that becomes a tarred road.

● At the corner, 50 yards after the beginning of the tarmac, you turn right and walk down to the harbour shore. This gives you a better view of the power station and a more delightful encounter with that thatched cottage at Wytch Passage. Venture as close as you dare to the remains of the jetty and then retrace your steps to the tarred road at the corner.

● This time you turn right, five yards before reaching the carriageway, through the first gate on your right. Then turn left through the next gate, in 50 yards, to pass immediately to the right of the outer regions of the main BP complex at what was Wytch Fir Pound. After following the security fence for a hundred yards the track the track then passes between more conventional fencing. Here and there you

glimpse ground-level piping and valves.

● Go through the iron gate at the end of this path and then turn right, through the second gate on your right-hand side. Going between the gorse and the brambles for 40 yards, this path initially heads away from the oilfield.

● Then you come to a field gate, to your left. Go through it and head left of centre to the gap in the hedgerow on the opposite side.

● Turn left in this field and keep the holly hedge to your left. In a hundred yards you turn left, through a gate, and then right at the farm track in six yards.

● Your course is now in a generally south-western direction and is rewarded by magical half-glimpses of Corfe Castle. Drop into the valley bottom and keep the stream to your right.

● This is the Corfe River and you come in 300 yards to the bridleway gate on Sharford Bridge. This splendid 17th century packhorse bridge had its parapets rebuilt by Dorset County Council after I created a fuss about its condition in 1971.

● On the other side you turn left of centre across the field, diagonally to the other hedgerow. Here you go through the centre gate and re-enter National Trust land. The bulrushes were teeming with warblers the day we researched the walk.

● Head south, towards the Purbeck Hills, but edge over into the right-hand corner of this pasture. Go through the gate and then immediately turn left, to enter a third field, and pass under a double line of electricity cables.

● Stop at this point and turn immediately right, through the gap in the gorse beside the closest of the power poles. In this field you turn left of centre, crossing it diagonally, and head towards the skyline.

● Go through the gateway in the top corner. Turn left in the next field, for just over 40 yards, and then continue into the following field.

● You enter it to the right of the "BP Pipeline" and a much older "CCC" stone which stands for "Corfe Castle Calcraft" and marked the boundary between Rempstone and Bankes estates.

● Follow the left-hand hedgerow down to the bottom corner of the field, towards the volcano-like silhouette of Crech Barrow. At the bottom there is a gate and the track leads straight ahead to another in 80 yards.

● This brings you onto the tarred road. Turn left to return to Scotland, in a hundred yards.

**Purbeck backdrop,
with Corfe centrepiece**

Moreton
& Clouds Hill

The restless spirit of Lawrence of Arabia — "the mystery man of the twentieth century" as he was dubbed by the newsreels — continues to stir the curiosity that he predicted. "After I'm dead they'll rattle my bones about," he wrote to Jock Chambers from his cottage retreat at Clouds Hill, concealed in a clump of rhododendrons a mile north of Bovington Camp, in 1929.

The manner of his departure, resulting from motor-cycle injuries received in a inexplicable accident involving two boy cyclists and a phantom black car, would be as enigmatic as all that had gone before.

Colonel Thomas Edward Lawrence, alias T. E. Shaw by deed poll and certainly to all who knew him in Dorset, was buried in Moreton cemetery on 21 May 1935. He was now national property once again, remembered as the hero of the Arab desert revolt, against the Turks in the Great war, and the author of its odyssey *The Seven Pillars of Wisdom*.

Winston Churchill led the procession from St Nicholas's church to the village graveyard. Other political notables included Lady Astor and the Iraqi chargé d'affairs. The literati were there in profusion — Florence Hardy, Jonathan Cape, Robert Graves, Augustus John, Siegfried Sassoon. Major General Archibald Wavell upstaged them all by arriving, from Aldershot, in an autogiro.

Those four locations — Clouds Hill, the accident spot, Moreton church and his grave — are visited on this four mile walk.

The church is a graceful gothic building, erected by landowner James Frampton in 1776 to replace a medieval church on the same grassy knoll. Its full dedication is to St Magnus the Martyr and St Nicholas of Myra, but it has been Nicholas who pulls rank.

On 8 October 1940 it was devastated by a German bomb but the post-war restoration has given it a set of windows that are among Dorset's major artistic creations of the century. Designed by Laurence Whistler and engraved in London between 1958 and 1984, under the direction of L. W. Legg at the Sand-blasting Decorative Glassworks, they are full of local allusions, including a memorial to wartime pilot Sergeant Bill Knowles who was killed on 10 May 1940.

"It is pleasant to have worked one's way around a church," Whistler commented on finishing what is regarded as the most complete example of his skills, incorporating the whole development of his style. He was at the peak of his profession, being elected the first president of the Guild of Grass Engravers in 1975.

Fourteen-year-old Prince Clarence, second son of the King of the Mosquitoes, was buried at Moreton in 1849. He was being educated in England at a time when friendly contacts between the natives of Belize and the British were causing resentment in Washington and disputes with the United States that continued through the 1850s.

The walk takes you across the widest shallows of anywhere on the River Frome, at a spot known as the Longbridge. From it, towards the far side, you have a view of Moreton House. It was built by Robert Frampton in 1580, burnt down in 1720, and rebuilt by James Frampton in 1744. Subsequent Framptons included the pananoid James who persecuted the Tolpuddle Martyrs, in 1834.

All paths on this circuit are firm and sandy, with the underlying geology churned by tank training in the vicinity of Bovington. Elsewhere the former heathland is almost totally covered by pine plantations, plus the rhododendrons that T. E. Lawrence was so keen on introducing.

The cottage at Clouds Hill, which he moved into in September 1923, was built for the gamekeeper of the Moreton Plantation and makes its debut on the Frampton estate records in 1808. It was presented to the nation, to the National Trust, by younger brother Arnold Walter Lawrence in 1938.

Current opening days, from April to the end of October, are Wednesday, Thursday, Friday, Sunday and Bank Holiday Mondays, all 2pm to 5pm. For the winter it is open only on Sunday, 1pm to 4pm.

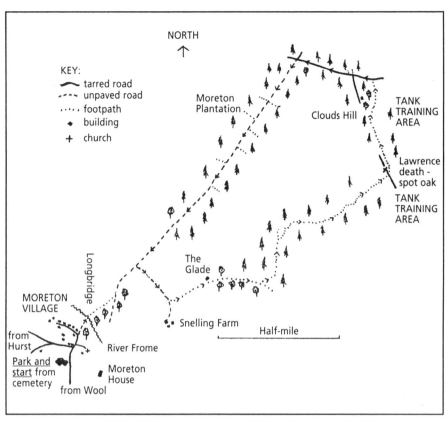

KEY:
━━━ tarred road
--- unpaved road
····· footpath
◆ building
✝ church

NORTH ↑

Moreton Plantation

Clouds Hill

TANK TRAINING AREA

Lawrence death-spot oak

TANK TRAINING AREA

Longbridge

The Glade

MORETON VILLAGE

Snelling Farm

Half-mile

from Hurst

River Frome

Park and start from cemetery

from Wool

Moreton House

Lawrence's effigy is in the Saxon church on Wareham's north wall

● Park and start from Moreton village. This is reached either from the A352 at Wool or Winfrith Newburgh, or by turning east off the B3390 at Hurst, which is between the River Frome and the Frampton Arms. There is a layby beside the classical lychgate at Moreton cemetery, 100 yards south of the junction at the centre of the village and opposite Moreton House (Ordnance Survey map reference SY 804 892).

● Go through the gate to find T. E. Lawrence's grave, which is at the end of the gravel path, between a wooden cross and the stone to Ethel Shrimpton who joined him in 1968. The marble tablets beneath the gate canopy are from the nearby Fir Hill column: "This Obelisk was erected in the Year 1784, by Captain JOHN HOULTON. As a publick Testimony of his Gratitude and Respect for the Memory of his much-esteemed and lamented Friend the late JAMES FRAMPTON Esq. of this Place."

● Turn left on leaving the gates. Turn right in 100 yards, beside the old school, "To the Church". Its turning is on the right in another 40 yards. Several of the gravestones are to staff from Moreton House, such as that in memory of Maria Jones: "A most faithful and attached servant for 50 years to James Frampton Esq. Died January 17th 1875. Aged 91."

● After seeing St Nicholas's and its superb Laurence Whistler windows you return to the lane. Continue along it, passing Moreton Post Office but not entering The Street of thatched cottages.

● Keep walking straight ahead, along the gravel track. This fords the River Frome, in 150 yards. Parallel to this, for you to cross, is the Longbridge. Moreton House is visible downstream as you near the far side. The other way, 25 yards to the left, is a circular 1940 pill-box with slits for the machine gunners.

● Continue straight ahead, along the gravel track. In 250 yards you turn left and cross a bridge. In another 250 yards you turn right.

● This untarred public road is signed by the Moreton estate to "Snelling Farm". In 400 yards you fork left, ignoring the little bridge and Snelling Farm. Pass the Glade Lodge and enter pine woodland that is fringed with gorse and rhododendron.

● In another 400 yards you again turn left, along a wide sandy track that then goes between fence posts. Fork right in 250 yards, on to a narrower path, and continue winding your way uphill. In a quarter of a mile you cross a stile into Army lands and turn left, along a gravel track. In another quarter of a mile, after walking beside the tank tracks, you emerge on the tarred road between Clouds Hill and Bovington Camp.

● Here, on the left side before widening, is the spot where T. E. Lawrence crashed his Brough Superior motor-cycle GW 2275. Cross to the parking area on the other side. At the left end of this is a commemorative oak planted by Lawrence's armoured car driver of the desert campaign: "NEAR THIS SPOT LAWRENCE OF ARABIA CRASHED ON HIS MOTOR CYCLE AND WAS FATALLY INJURED 13 MAY 1935. THIS TREE WAS PLANTED ON 13 MAY 1983 BY MR. TOM BEAUMONT WHO SERVED WITH LAWRENCE IN ARABIA."

● Exit from the parking area in the corner eight yards east of the tree, midway between the public road and the Army's wide tank road.

● Climb the bank and follow the fence, keeping the tank road to your right, on the other side of it. Off-putting as it seems, this is a public path. It formerly went through half a holly bush but is now open and usable, courtesy my secateurs.

● In 400 yards the fence brings you to a sandy gulley beside a rhododendron thicket which smothers the seven acres of Lawrence's Clouds Hill that are owned by the National Trust. On the top the track forks left, away from the fence, and descends beside a Ministry of Defence bye-laws sign, through heather to a tarred road.

● Turn left, in 150 yards, to see Clouds Hill Cottage, which is on the left in another 150 yards. Then return to the junction and continue left, towards "Tincleton 3½, Dorchester 8¾".

● In 400 yards you come to a crossroads. Turn left here, beside the overgrown site of North Lodge, down an untarred public road which descends in a straight line through Forestry Commission plantations.

● It leads towards Snelling Farm, bringing you in a mile to the track where you turned off earlier.

● Now continue straight ahead, to cross the bridge, and fork right. Return via the Longbridge to Moreton Post Office and your car.

Badbury Rings
& Lodge Farm

Renewal and rediscovery have gathered pace since the National Trust took the famous Badbury Rings beauty spot into its care in 1982. It came with the rest of the 16,000-acre estate of Ralph Bankes and was full of management headaches. Cars were about the only effective means of scrub control and the earthworks were being gouged by the feet of thousands of visitors, leaving white gashes of exposed chalk.

These days there are still some 200,000 visitors a year but the parking has been brought into the realms of sanity and most of the bushes have been cleared.

The work has uncovered hedge-sized banks in the interior of Badbury Rings, well inside its massive encircling fortifications, that were the enclosure of an extensive Neolithic causewayed camp dating to between 3500 and 3000 BC.

The Rings are much more recent, being a major multi-vallate Iron Age hill-fort comprising three sets of ramparts and outer ditches. It was built and extended over a considerable period, with the forerunner of the inner bank being dated to about 700 BC, and the centre ring to 400 BC and the outer circle to AD 40.

Slightly oblong in plan, though visibly appearing as circular, the concentric banks enclose about eighteen acres of rounded hilltop. The defences would have been palisaded and are engineered for slingstone warfare with the additional height of the inner banks giving the fire-power advantage to the defenders. They would also have had plenty of shot as the hilltop clays of the Reading beds are peppered with a natural supply of slingstone pebbles.

The hill-fort has well preserved outworks and entrances. It was a major fortress of the Durotrigic peoples that saw its last warfare in AD 44-45 when Vespasian's Second Legion started the campaign that conquered the West of England for the Roman Empire.

Their marching camp lies on the other side of the Wimborne to Blandford road at Crab Farm. Finds of ballista bolts, fired by Roman artillery machines, have come from around the fort and indicate that it was besieged. Spears and swords have also been found.

There is no evidence, however, beyond scholarly wishful thinking, to link Badbury Rings with the great victory of the legendary British leader, Arthur. His epic battle of Mount Badon, which held back the Saxon advance for 30 years, probably took place near Bath.

Two dewponds, restored in 1984 by young people working with the Prince's Trust, date back to prehistoric times and form the only standing water for a mile and a half.

Bada's Castle, named for a Dark Ages war-leader, has been the name of the fortifications from AD 710 onwards.

Badbury Warren came into existence when medieval warreners utilised the ancient defences as a stockade for rabbit breeding, a valuable resource following their introduction by the Normans, until inevitable escapes led to their general mass colonisation of the entire countryside.

The next short-term name was Badbury Clump, with the planting of skyline trees on what was open downland until the 18th century. These Scots pines were set out as a piece of landscape gardening, with five vistas radiating as grassy glades from a central viewing area. This feature, since infiltrated by hardwoods, was restored in the 1980s and a bronze topograph mounted on a stone plinth. Adjacent concrete footings held the stays of a wartime radio mast, erected on the summit of the hill, at 327 feet above sea level.

Unimproved downland around Badbury Rings covers a major scattering of Bronze Age and Roman antiquities and has yielded a considerable quantity of finds. The visible remains are the round barrow burial mounds and the roads which converge from Hamworthy, Dorchester, Hod Hill, Bath and Salisbury at an important junction in the form of a double triangle between the northern rampart of the hill-fort and the western end of what is now King Down Drove.

Of the roads which can be traced on the ground, the best preserved is a section of Ackling Dyke from the B3082 at its junction with New Road, extending half a mile north-east to the parish boundary hedge.

This carriageway survives as a bank 35 feet wide and 4 feet high, flanked by side-banks and ditches 120 feet apart.

Between the entrances to the downland and the Rings stood the small town of Vindocladia which took its name from the fort's White Ditches. Occasional disturbances have revealed stone walls and finds of beads, late Roman coinage and black-burnished pottery. There were administrative buildings at the north-west edge of the settlement.

Relict colonies of chalkland flowers have spread since the National Trust onslaught on the scrub that had engulfed Badbury Rings and much of its immediate surroundings. Subsequently ash trees on the ramparts have been cut as they recover to ten feet and the grazing régime is a flock of Portland sheep from Calke Abbey, descendants of those said to have been shipwrecked on the Chesil Beach during the Spanish Armada.

Thirty-four pairs of yellow-hammers nested on the south side of the hill-fort in 1991 and apparently endorsed the progressive policy of scrub control. Some 480 workers sweltered in the tropical summer of 1984 to set back the clock, restoring the Rings to its appearance of 1914, and repairing 139 "erosion scars" caused by human feet as well as attacking the natural regeneration.

Meanwhile, the hurricane of January 1990 downed 41 trees in the famous Beech Avenue that was planted for two miles along the main road by William John Bankes in 1835 as an anniversary gift for his mother. "There is one for each day of the year," to quote the guidebooks — but there are two sides to an avenue and one has an extra tree for leap year. In fact the total was 731 trees and it has now been doubled as the National Trust has established two parallel rows of young replacements set back from the original line on each side.

These will be pollarded after fifteen to twenty year's growth, so that they match their predecessors. Coach drivers continue to perpetrate the myth that there is a gold sovereign under each of those; Dorset men had a national reputation for being slow in the head but they were never quite that thick.

The new trees do have some decorative metal, in the form of traditional Kingston Lacy-style iron tree guards with distinctively flared tops, made on the estate.

Lodge Farm stands close to the Wimborne end of the famous trees. Restoration and research since Stephen Burden took over this dilapidated farmhouse in 1977 have revealed that it was the pivotal building of the medieval Kingston Lacy estate. It was built as a first-floor great hall and solar, perhaps for John of Gaunt, in the late fourteenth century. Philippa Oakes-Ash has told me its history.

This was a hunting lodge, both for the adjoining 300-acre deer park at Kingston Lacy and a chase which extended for twenty-one miles and was six miles wide. The house was semi-defensive; secure with high walls of iron-impregnated gritstone from the heath and glazing bars set into traceried windows of Chilmark and limestone. These, on the ground floor, had only single lights. Upstairs, a magnificent oak screen divides the hall and solar.

Other discoveries have included earlier foundations and fragments of medieval murals. Most of the architectural features of the house had been plastered over or rendered in concrete. There were clues to its history, such as chamfered beams, set on stone corbels, and other moulded timbers but, at the time Burden moved in, it had slipped in the estate's tenancy roll to the status of surplus cottage and was only one stage away from demolition.

The prairie fields nearby include 268 acres of registered common land that were put under the plough as a result of wartime agricultural regulations that came into force in 1940. The National Trust has inherited something of a dilemma under its own statutory requirements for the care of common land and, arguably, should think about de-fencing King Down.

Common land registered unit CL70 extends for two miles, northwards from the east end of the Beech Avenue. Some grass has been re-established, around two Bronze Age burial mounds which are warrior graves dating to between 2100 and 1600 BC, but it is a different landscape entirely from its pre-war appearance as an open sheep range.

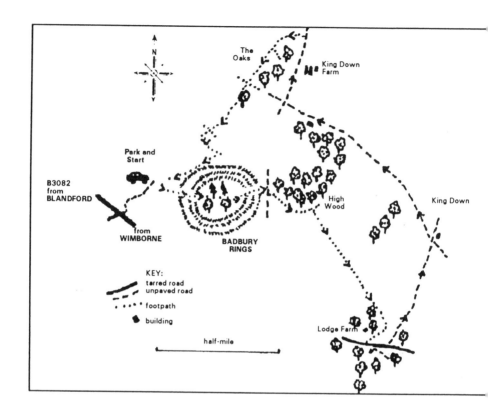

● This four mile walk is on firm chalky footpaths across the Badbury Rings downland and its surrounding fields and woods. Park and start from the car-park which is signposted off the B3082, Wimborne to Blandford road, four miles north-west of Wimborne Minster.

● From here you walk across the grassy causeway of the Roman road into the main entrance of the hill-fort. After three sets of ditches and banks you enter the wooden interior. Pass the dewponds and walk up to the topograph which is mounted on stone at the centre of the five glades.

● Take the south-eastern one, which is shown as pointing towards Lodge Farm, Wimborne Minster, Kingston Lacy and the Isle of Wight. After crossing the remainder of the interior of the fort you climb on to the inner rampart and turn left along it.

● Then turn right through the opening in the triple earthworks.

You are now heading towards High Wood. As you approach the trees there is a stile to the left of the gate.

● Cross the stile and turn right along the track, but only for ten yards, before turning left to walk beside the wood. The trees are to your left, around the corner of the wood, you then turn right.

● A straight path follows the hedge, which you keep to your right, downhill for more than half a mile in the general direction of Lodge Farm and Kingston Lacy House, both of which can be glimpsed through the trees.

● The track bends to the right to pass Lodge Farm and then you turn left at the end of Beech Avenue, beside the main road. Turn left again in a hundred yards, on to a farm road that is signposted as a bridleway.

● You pass over the "BP PIPELINE" and come to a crossroads of farm tracks in half a mile, immediately before a barn.

● Turn left here and walk for a mile along King Down Drove. This passes High Wood and a keeper's cottage and you then come to another crossroads of farm tracks, in the dip.

● Turn right and walk past King Down Farm, which is to your right. Admire the National Trust's renovation of the tiled barn, behind the modern monstrosities.

● Continue straight ahead beside a wood called The Oaks. On the brow of the hill, 300 yards after the barns, you turn left.

● This woodland path, through The Oaks, bends gradually to the left, below more ash than oak. Keep walking straight ahead, with the main part of the wood to your left and fields just visible beyond the perimeter fence to your right.

● Keep straight on at the crossroads near the southern edge of the wood, where it tapers into a shelter-belt.

● Go over the brow of the hill, from which Badbury Rings returns to view, left of centre. In the dip you re-enter the unspoilt chalk downland and turn left, after the scrub, to walk up to the causeway or agger of the Roman road. This lies just beyond the sheep fence, about 50 yards in front of the ramparts of the hill-fort. Turn right along the ancient road (with your back to Salisbury and London) and head for Dorchester and your car. The latter is within half a mile.

Stourpaine
& Hod Hill

The acquisition in 1984 by the National Trust of the 67-acre top of Hod
Hill, together with its ancient banks and ditches on the south and west
sides of the magnificent hill-fort overlooking the River Stour, created
a delightful four mile walk from the village of Stourpaine. In 1985 an
appeal raised a further £9,000 to buy the other banks and ditches. "The
National Trust has gone all out for the remaining two banks," Gill Raikes
told us. "All who have given money have shown they understand the
importance of the Trust owning Hod Hill. Its unspoilt character,
beautiful views and historic past have appealed to the people of Dorset."

Our walk begins from Stourpaine, the older part of which was missed
by the lower Blandford to Shaftesbury main road and is a charming mix
of flint, brick and thatch. The village lies on the A350 three miles north
of Blandford.

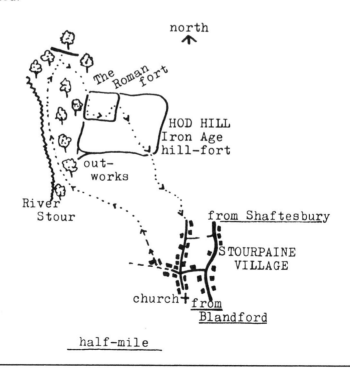

• Turn off the A350 (Shaston Road) into Stourpaine village at the turning (South Holme) beside the White Horse public house. Park on the left-hand side towards the end, or around the corner (Manor Road) on the stretch leading up to the church (Ordnance Survey map reference ST 860 096).

• The walk starts from the crossroads at the junction of South Holme with Manor Road and you follow the fourth road (Havelins) towards the fields. Walk along the tarred section to the little bridge and then turn right (ignoring the main lane) into an old double-hedged muddy trackway that passes between two thatched cottages and climbs the slope of Hod Hill. The track is signposted: "BRIDLEWAY TO HANFORD". The southern ramparts of Hod Hill form the skyline. The track skirts the foot of Hod and towards the far end you can see the triangular-shaped outworks that defended its most vulnerable corner. Here the track narrows to a footpath and descends through a wood on to a terrace that follows the banks of the River Stour. Hod's steepest side rises to your right — the ideal canvas for an Uffington or Cerne-type hill figure if every chalkland fort had its own emblem. The slope is now a damp ash-wood smothered in hart's tongue ferns. There are even some birnest orchids. It is one of the prettiest paths in Dorset. The best trees, a few London plane and some clumps of beech, are near the end where you look across to Dorset's only yew-wood, on the northern foothills of Hambledon.

• You approach a tarred road. The mound opposite, planted with young trees, conceals a superb 18th century ice-house, which is about eighteen feet in diameter with a domed brick-roof and an entrance at the top (definitely out-of-bounds as there is an instant twenty foot drop — but certainly worthy of a National Trust appeal one day in the future).

• Our path does not cross the tarred road but turns right from the riverside track at a point 75 feet from the road. Climb up the usually muddy slope to the hunting gate ("Please shut the gate") and climb to the top of the hill. Head just to the right of the high point, a bit right of centre by the side of the wood. In 1985 wooden stakes beside the first bank set out the area which the National Trust was negotiating to purchase.

• The entrance to the Iron Age hill-fort is through the banks at its corner, into the area which the Romans later commandeered for their own fort to suppress the natives on Cranborne Chase. Inside the entrance, to the left you will see a series of scooped depressions: these were a quarry ditch for the Iron Age embankment rather than a defence.

• Follow the side overlooking the Stour valley. This way you get the best view over the Blackmore Vale (above the wood through which you walked) where the precipitous side needed only a token bank. This has for a number of years been leased to the Dorset Naturalists Trust and the hill is a site of special scientific interest with horseshoe vetch, devil's bit scabious, autumn gentian, clustered bellflower and five species of orchids — bee, frog, pyramidal, twayblade, fragrant and common spotted. The National Trust intends discouraging scrub from invading the grassland but cricket expert Bernard C. Pickard puts in a special plea for the retention of

Hod's blackberry bushes: "They are the home of the great green bush cricket, which is a very impressive insect and the bramble is all-important for it, and for a number of other things. It supports a whole community of wildlife." The grassland has its phalanxes of butterflies, including the marbled white, marsh fritillary and the chalkhill and other blues. The banks have never been ploughed or doused with chemicals but much of the interior was ploughed in Victorian times and during the Second World War. In the valley, the side arches are visible of the bridge that carried the Somerset and Dorset Railway across the river from 1863 until 1966.

• Towards the lower side of the hill, but some distance from the corner, four pairs of lesser banks and ditches join the outer bank from the interior of the fort. These are the earthworks of the Roman fort built by Vespasian's Second Legion Augusta after the invasion of AD43. Walk along them to observe the neat entrance, guarded by a low ramp on which stood an artillery piece firing ballistabolts. Note at the corner the smooth and precise turn that is made by each bank and ditch, in particular the central gullies, and the fact that the inner ditch is really two ditches with a hump in the middle. These to an attacker, would have been the killing fields of Hod. The Roman earthwork on Hod has been described by me in *Romans in Britain* (Heinemann, 1983) and I'll quote that rather than try to figure it all out again: "This work was based upon a simple but lethal ditch system overlooked by an inner rampart. It was a ten foot high wall with a walk along the top, timber reinforcements, and sides made from stacks of turf. The ditches lie on the outside and take up a level strip ninety feet wide and five feet deep. It started with a vertical drop but then offered a gentle rise towards the fort. This was a trap — the intruder was offered an unhindered run across 55 feet of open ground. Suddenly, he came to a previously unnoticed ditch, intended to throw an attacker on to the rocks and break his leg. This, and another ditch, lay directly under the shadow of the wall and escape would have been impossible for any who fell. Those who turned to run back to the outermost ditch were also in a trap. The first ditch they had leapt effortlessly was impossible to jump back across. Escape was blocked by a vertical outer face, within the thirty-yard killing range of hand-thrown missiles from the fort wall. As the enemy tried to scramble up the rock face their backs would have been open targets for spears thrown from the rampart. The defences encouraged the approach and confidence of the attacker, and then kept him in a field of fire from which there was no retreat. It was the intellectual side of warfare, compared with the sheer bulk of their prehistoric predecessors."

● Leave by the next entrance. Ian Richmond's excavations in the 1950s uncovered the headquarters building, hospital, stables, latrines and other features of the Roman fort but there is nothing to enable you to locate them on the ground. The more interesting course is to go downhill into the middle of the Durotrigic hill-fort. You are facing the rolling corn fields of Cranborne Chase, which in the Roman period as now were the grainlands of Britain and Europe. You cross some slight depressions of hut circles. Some were excavated by Richmond who showed that the Romans had attacked them before capturing the fort, firing flaming arrows deep into the encampment — perhaps the inmates surrendered, or maybe as in the case of Maiden Castle they were then put to the sword for their resistance. So far no war cemetery has been found here but it is strange that we find peace in a place that has probably seen far more brutality than most of us, with a bit of luck, will ever encounter. The name "Hod" also has Celtic roots and in Welsh means "quiet". Look out for one hut circle to the left of the cattle track (or sheep path if the National Trust have their way) about a hundred yards before the stile. This is the best of the group, though none is as clearly visible as those at Abbotsbury Castle, and its interior is largely covered in nettles. It is 25 feet in diameter, which would have been a large building, and its entrance faces north-east — away from the prevailing wind. This is noticeable as a slight depression with longer grass.

● A break in the banks of the hill-fort leads to a double-hedged trackway which has National Trust signs. The biggest lettering reads: "NO METAL DETECTORS". They are not only unauthorised but would be illegal as the whole hill is a scheduled ancient monument. Most of the finds from Hod, namely the Victorian Durden collection and Richmond's own, are in the British Museum. Over the years some in private hands have been discussed in *The Dorset County Magazine* including a magnificent skillet-handle featuring the Celtic god Nodons, with numerous of his attributes being depicted (issue 50), and a raven's head which is also cast in bronze. These are the finest of all the finds from Hod Hill. They came into the collection of Richard Hattatt of Spencer Road, New Milton, author of *Ancient and Romano-British Brooches* (Dorset Publishing Co, £25) which is the textbook on its subject and includes a section on Hod-type brooches which take their name from the hill because of the number that were found here.

● The hedgerows of the trackway downhill to Stourpaine are smothered in old man's beard, the wild clematis, and the banks have been dug by badgers. At the foot of the hill in wintertime you may have to divert to the right (taking

---

care not to do any damage to either the fence or the corn) as the footpath has literally become the bed of the River Iwerne.

● You come into the village at the appropriately named Brook Cottage and the land becomes Manor Road, bringing you to your car. The cottage by the corner is a splendid example of an historic structural defect — the brickwork of its front wall bowing out at ceiling level. The problem was solved by four contemporary buttresses.

A Dorset farmhouse

Fontmell Down
& Melbury Beacon

National Trust ownership of the high-rise corner of Cranborne Chase now encompasses more than a square mile of the highest escarpments and best combes of the Dorset chalklands. Trust land-buying started here with 149 acres of Fontmell Down in 1979 and expanded through the 1980s into the status of an "estate" that stretches across 725 acres of unspoilt uplands.

A tongue of dry valley, known locally as the Devil's Plat, and alternatively as the Silent Valley, extends deep into the Chase, to reach the Ox Drove on the Wiltshire boundary near Win Green. The Trust's holding also includes two much cherished viewpoints — Melbury Beacon above Shaftesbury, and that famous vista of the Blackmore Vale down Longcombe Bottom. This western edge of the Trust's land is explored here in a five-mile walk which also brings in Spread Eagle Hill and Clubmen's Down.

The latter takes its name from a gathering of 3,000 club-wielding protesters, rallied on 25 May 1645 by Rev. Thomas Bravell, the rector of Compton Abbas. Their message for King Charles and Oliver Cromwell was that the Civil war had dragged on too long and that both sides should leave them alone. The Clubmen of Dorset and Wiltshire moved on to Badbury Rings and then to another ancient encampment, Hambledon Hill, where they were surprised by units of the Parliamentary army. It was an unequal contest which left 12 of the clubmen dead and the rest locked for the night in Shroton church. The following morning they promised to disband and were allowed to return to their homes.

Older history is etched into the ground at both of the Fontmell and Melbury high-points. The principal earthworks are Iron Age linear cross-dykes that defended settlements. There is also a Saxon ranch boundary that ran for more than a mile on the Shaftesbury side of Melbury Hill. The actual summit, Melbury Beacon, carried warning fires in 1588 for the Spanish Armada, and was brought back into action in 1804 when French invasion was feared.

Down below, also on the course of this walk, is the remains of Thomas Bravell's church. It was reduced to just the 15th-century tower in 1867, when the new Victorian church was built half a mile away in the main village. The old churchyard is guarded by geese and remains charmingly rustic.

There is also naturalist's countryside. In Longcombe Bottom the Dorset Wildlife Trust — or whatever it calls itself, for it has gone through three name changes during the completion of this book — manages an extensive down and woodland reserve that partially overlaps the National Trust land. The obscenity, as bad as any new road, was an obtrusive cutting through the southern woods, in the autumn of 1994. That said, the joint holding it is notable for several types of skipper and blue butterfly, plus a breeding bird list that includes nightingale, turtle dove, skylark and several species of warblers.

Above, they have to share the sky with an interesting assortment of biplanes and piston-engined monoplanes that take off into the vale from Compton Abbas airfield, which has become Dorset's main leisure aerodrome.

Looking the other way, sheep-cropped turf reveals an extensive flora between the ant-hills. It is herb-rich with clustered bellflower, scabious, early gentian, hairbell, horseshoe vetch, knapweed, hairy violet, fragrant orchid and bee orchid. I also found rest harrow, milkwort, hawkweed and quaking grass.

Compton Abbas

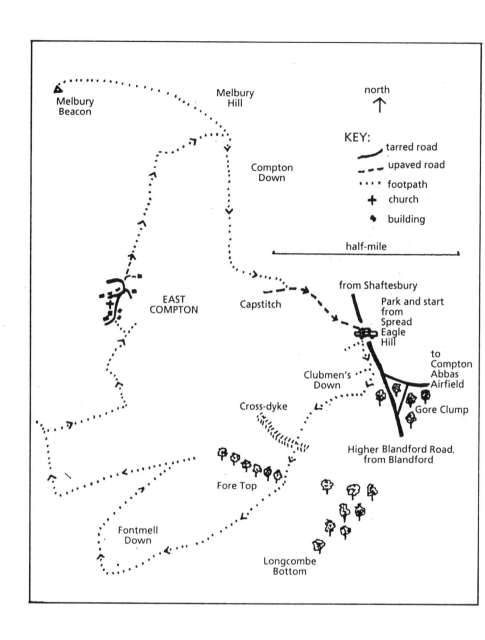

Melbury Beacon

Melbury Hill

Compton Down

north

KEY:
— tarred road
- - - upaved road
· · · · footpath
✝ church
◆ building

half-mile

EAST COMPTON

Capstitch

from Shaftesbury

Park and start from Spread Eagle Hill

to Compton Abbas Airfield

Clubmen's Down

Gore Clump

Cross-dyke

Higher Blandford Road, from Blandford

Fore Top

Fontmell Down

Longcombe Bottom

Access for walkers is from the Higher Blandford Road, which is the C13 hilltop route between Blandford and Shaftesbury. Park in the National Trust car-park near the top of Spread Eagle Hill, opposite the west side of Compton Abbas Airfield (OS map reference ST 886 187).Walk up the hill, beside the fence rather than on the tarmac, to the junction in 200 yards. Here cross the stile into the main expanse of Fontmell Down. The top part includes Clubmen's Down. Walk left of centre, towards the outstanding view down Longcombe Bottom and into the Blackmore Vale.

● Descend to the fence and then turn right, following it around the rim of the valley. In half a mile, after the double banks of the prehistoric cross-dykes, you reach a hilltop shelter belt. Cross the stile, to the left of the beech trees and beside a gate. Then continue straight ahead, keeping the fence to your left. In another half-mile you come to a gate and stile on the skyline. This spur-end of the down gives you a panoramic view across the vale. The surrounding heights extend from Bulbarrow to the western hills, and in the north to the woods at Duncliffe and Alfred's Tower.

● On the other side of the stile turn right, initially toward Melbury Beacon. Then head right of centre, following the fence up into the corner of the Fore Top, to the left of the scrub. Turn left, across the stile between the gates. On the other side turn left again, descending along a track that passes a parish boundary stone in 50 yards. You are heading for the lakes at Manor Farm, Fontmell Magna.

● At the bottom of the escarpment there is a gate and the path leaves the Trust's land. Continue straight ahead, following the left-hand fence into the next corner of the pasture. Then turn right, keeping the fence to your left. Cross the stile beside the gate. Continue straight ahead for 180 yards to the next gates. Here turn right, technically having gone through the first gate and then right through the second. From here a second bridleway crosses the field, at ninety degrees to the first path.

● On the other side you approach a metal gate but do not go through it. Instead turn left, through a second gate and into a length of double-hedged trackway. This brings you to more gates. The bridleway continues ahead, through the third gate, and then bends to the right to follow the hedge towards the hamlet of East Compton. After the next two gates turn left, up a muddy track which brings you to the tarred road. Turn right, passing Greenstones and the tower of St Mary's church. Note the horse-mounting block beside the old gate, clumps of old box bushes, and the square steps which are the plinth of a mediaeval preaching cross among the gravestones.

● Continue along the lane, beside more greensand architecture at East End, and then fork left, following the stone wall around the corner. In 20 yards, opposite the beech trees, turn right, along a bridleway that is signed to "MELBURY ABBAS". This follows the left-hand fence, across level ground at the foot of the escarpment.

● After the gate you cross a pasture. The path then bends to the right, through a gate and back into National Trust land. You are now tackling Melbury Hill, up a rising chalky track terraced into the hillside. Turn left as you approach the top, keeping on this side of the fence, and make the final assault on Melbury Beacon.

It is a half-mile climb that brings you to 862 feet above sea level and a view over Shaftesbury. The Saxon ranch boundary ditch runs along the slope above Melbury Abbas village.

● After seeing the ancient beacon barrow and the view from the triangulation pillar, turn round and follow the fence back to the field gate on the hilltop — above your initial climb from East Compton. Make sure you are still on the same side of the fence as the trackway. Now follow the fence at the top of the slope, towards Fontmell Down. The fence is on your left and East Compton lies in the valley to the right. The hillside is Compton Down.

● In half a mile, after bending to the left and into the next valley, you approach an old chalkpit. Two hundred yards before reaching this, drop down to a stile in the right-hand hedgerow. The steps bring you down to a stony lane, which is known as Capstitch. Turn left, uphill towards Compton Abbas Airfield — into the usual flight-path for take-off — and return to your car, which is at the top of the escarpment.

INDEX

[Trust-owned properties
being signified by **bold type**]

A

Abbotsbury	31
Alfred's Tower	69
Anchor Inn	18, 20

B

Badbury Rings	54 - 59, 66
Ballard Down	37 - 41
Barrowland Farm	30
Beech Avenue	56, 57
Blackmore Vale	62, 69
Bovington Camp	53
Bradford Abbas	16
Bridport	24, 25, 31
Broom Cliff	14
Bull Inn	31
Burton Bradstock	31

C

Cain's Folly	11, 25
Cann Harbour	16
Capstitch	70
Castle Mill Farm	27, 29
Champernhayes Lodge	10
Chardown Hill	11, 13
Charmouth	13 - 15, 20
Chesil Beach	5, 14, 31, 33, 36
Chideock	17 - 21
Clay Lane	35
Clouds Hill	49 - 53
Clubmen's Down	66
Compton Abbas	66, 67, 70
Compton Down	70
Coney's Castle	7, 9
Corfe Castle	5, 42, 44, 47
Corner, The	16
Cove, The	16
Cranborne Chase	62, 63, 66

D

Dalwood Common	6
Devil's Plat	66

Downhouse Farm	23, 25
Duncliffe Hill	69

E

East Compton	70
Eggardon Hill	27 - 30
Eype Down	22 - 26

F

Fair House	5
Fir Hill	52
Fishpond Bottom	7 - 10
Fontmell Down	66 - 70
Fontmell Magna	69
Fore Top	69
Frampton Arms	52
Frome, River	49, 52

G

Gipsies End	9
Godlingston Hill	39
Golden Cap	11 - 21, 24, 32
Great Coombe	9
Green Pond	46

H

Halfway Inn	44
Hambledon Hill	66
Hanford	61
Hardown Hill	11
Hawkchurch	5, 10
High Wood	59
Higher Coombe	9
Hod Hill	60 - 65

I

Iwerne, River	65

K

King Down	59
Kingston Lacy	57, 58
Kitwells Cliff	14
Knackers Hole	35
Knoll, The	35, 36

L

Lambert's Castle Hill   5 - 10
Langdon Hill   11, 20
Lawrence of Arabia's Cottage   49, 53
Limekiln Hill   31, 36
Little Coombe   9
Lodge Farm   54 - 59
Longbridge, The   52
Longcombe Bottom   66, 67, 69
Lyme Bay   11 - 21, 29
Lyme Regis   6, 8, 14, 15

M

Manor Farm, Fontmell Magna   69
Manor Farm, Studland   37, 41
Marsh Farm   16
Marshwood   5
Marshwood Vale   7, 27, 29, 35
Melbury Beacon   66 - 70
Melbury Hill   66, 70
Mill Lane   20, 21
Monkton Wyld   10
Monument Coppice   15
Morcombelake   12, 14
Moreton   49 - 53

N

New Mills   42

O

Oaks, The   59
Old Harry Rocks   37 - 41
Ower Quay   45
Ox Drove   66
Pilsdon Pen   5
Pinnacle, The   37
Poole Harbour   40, 42 - 48
Portland   5, 14, 16, 22
Powerstock Castle   29
Powerstock Common   27 - 30
Puncknowle   31 - 36
Purbeck   5, 16, 37-48

Q

Quarry Hill   21

R

Rempstone Forest   45, 46
Ridge   14

S

St. Gabriel's Bridge   13
St. Gabriel's Water   14
St. Gabriel's Wood   20
Scotland   42 - 48
Seatown   16 - 21
Shaftesbury   70
Sharford Bridge   42, 45, 47
Silent Valley   66
Snelling Farm   52
Spence Farm   10
Spread Eagle Hill   66, 69
Stanton St. Gabriel   12, 13, 16, 20
Stonebarrow Hill   11 -15
Stour, River   61, 62
Studland   37 - 41
Swanage   37 - 41
Swyre   31 - 36

T

Tempest Cottage   5 - 10
Thorncombe Beacon   22 - 26
Toller Down   6
Trevitt's Corner   10
Turf-Rick Rock   37

U

Ulwell Gap   37, 39

W

Watch House   19
West Bay   24, 26
West Bexington   31
Western Patches   16
Whetley   29, 30
Win Green   66
Woodsford Castle   39
Wootton Fitzpaine   10
Wootton Manor   5
Wynford Eagle   28, 30
Wytch   42 - 47